THE SKILLS OF INTERVIEWING

The skills of interviewing

A guide for managers and trainers

Leslie Rae

Gower

Published by
Gower Publishing Company Limited,
Gower House,
Croft Road,
Aldershot,
Hants GU11 3HR,
England.

Rae, Leslie.
  The skills of interviewing: a
  guide for managers and trainers
  1. Employment interviewing
  I. Title
  658.3'1124   HF5549.5.16

  ISBN 0–566–02722–4

Printed and bound in Great Britain by
Biddles Ltd, Guildford and King's Lynn

Contents

Preface

This book is aimed both at managers who are in charge of and responsible for staff, at whatever level, and who have frequent interview contact with them, and also at those very staff so that they might know what to expect or require from their bosses in various interactive situations. It is also aimed at trainers who need to be aware of the developmental needs of managers and the techniques which are useful to them as interviewers. But above all the book is intended to enable managers to start learning about interviews without having to go on a training course; although having seen what is required, this may be the next step. Attendance on that training course will be more useful and fulfilling with the background knowledge provided in the book.

The specific objectives are to describe as comprehensively as possible the techniques which can be recommended in the majority of interviews, whatever their nature, and also to suggest appropriate action in a number of specific types of representative interviews.

In view of the method of treatment adopted in the book, it can be used as a form of self-instructional guide to interviewing for managers and supervisors. Not, may I quickly add, as the only training aid to the subject. As with any aspect of human behaviour, the only way to learn how to behave is to behave and then analyse this behaviour. Unfortunately this pragmatic approach has its own problems, even if the practical events are preceded by the reading, understanding and commitment to a book of this nature. When managers new to interactions with staff decide to improve their skills in interviewing, the natural first step is to read about techniques, methods and structure; then to decide on a process which will suit their personalities and personal preferences. Unfortunately the usual next step is the real live interview with a real live person who has a problem, need or grievance. In this situation, even with considerable preparation, all may not go well and the theoretical approach may not suffice. At best, the interviewee may decide that the interviewer is simply inept or unhelpful and terminate the interview. At worst a nasty incident could arise which could sour any future relationship.

Part I of the book describes the various techniques of conducting effective interviews – basic questioning; the structure of interviews based on the viewpoints held by different people; the levels of questioning and the discipline of listening; the interview as a problem to be solved; and a systematic approach to planning. This is followed by a summary of the training available to managers to acquire these skills, skills which can often be appreciated by imagining oneself in the interviewee's place. Consequently the latter part of this chapter demonstrates some of the problems encountered 'on the receiving end'.

Part II of the book describes in some detail the application of these principles in specific types of interviews. The interviews described are what might be considered as the standard interview units, on the basis of which, with minor modifications, we can tackle other types.

An increasing number of women are entering the supervisory and managerial ranks, at all levels. I support this trend wholeheartedly, but for the sake of simplicity in the book I use the generally acceptable he, his, him, himself etc. rather than the clumsy she/he or the even clumsier plural format.

Leslie Rae

Acknowledgements

I should like to acknowledge my gratitude to the many people who have suffered being interviewed by me, and conversely those who have made me suffer in the reverse position as interviewee. They have given me the opportunity to learn and practise the techniques recommended in this book, and to observe the styles, good and bad, practised on me.

My thanks must also go to my wife Susan for her encouragement, patience, forbearance and advice, and to my two young sons Alexander and Oliver who have contributed to 'Daddy's new book' by actually allowing me to write it.

Gower Publishing have a special place in my gratitude for their renewed support both in helping me to prepare the manuscript for publication and for wanting to publish it, an indication of their continuing faith in me. I should particularly like to thank Malcolm Stern and Ellen Keeling for all their hard work.

LR

Part I

Interview Techniques

1 The manager's role in interviewing

It is often said that one of the prime responsibilities of a manager is the training and development of his staff. This must be just as true as the responsibility for achieving his prescribed tasks, since, if the manager's subordinates are inefficient and ineffective and are not helped to increase their efficiency and effectiveness, the task may not be achieved. If it is achieved it is at too great a cost, or at the risk of other effects many of which are less obvious. However, developing relationships which will assist the manager to achieve any aims of training and development calls for positive efforts on the part of the manager.

Many efforts will be subconscious or unconscious interactions between managers and their staff – the natural affinity between people – provided that the manager wants to develop relationships and has the ability to do so.

The last twenty years or so have seen the development of many attitudinal changes, although the staff relations 'revolution' is far from complete. One such development has been the introduction of the 'open door' policy in which the manager's door is always open to his staff – actually open in some cases, a figure of speech in others. This has replaced the boss-subordinate relationship which existed in the vast majority of cases for many years in which the boss was not only behind a closed door, but was rarely seen.

The manager should become involved only in problems which nobody else can solve and as a result managerial skill is used when it is needed. This also releases a considerable

amount of time which otherwise would be used
inefficiently.

PROBLEM OWNERSHIP

Involvement, however, does not mean shouldering the
problems of others; rather it means putting the problem
ownership where it should be. One way of limiting the
problem load is to ensure that the ownership of the
problem, whenever possible or desirable, is transferred
back to the worker. This necessitates effective counselling
which will be described more fully later. For the moment
let us take the case of the worker who approaches the
manager (or indeed the supervisor) with a work-related
problem. The senior has two options, or three where a
negative response is intended. In the latter case, a
draconian approach is taken simply by sending away the
seeker of aid. There may be some justification in this, but
such action can produce poor manager-worker
relationships. The worker, having been rejected, may say
to himself: 'If the boss can't be bothered with this problem
I have, why should I be?'. Consequently both the
relationship and the work suffer and there is the even
greater danger that problems about which the manager
ought to be aware, are not brought to his notice.

Of the two more positive options, the first will be much
less appropriate than the other, although easier to take. If
the manager is asked to solve a problem, the move by the
worker can be looked upon as a compliment by the
solution-seeker and can be a positive boost to the
manager's ego: 'I am recognized as the authority/the
expert/god, so I shall accept this role and solve the
problem'. With this ego-building attitude in mind the
manager, having heard the problem description, decides
on the solution and gives this to the worker with the preface
'If I were you I would . . .' or 'What you have to do is . . .'.

There will be obvious occasions when it is necessary for
the manager to solve the problem, since he may be the only
one capable of doing so. But there are dangers, particularly

if the manager becomes fixed in this approach. The worker, having been given the tablet of stone, may go away rejecting the solution internally and seething because it has to be put into operation – the manager has so decreed. The decision did not fit in with what the worker wanted to do or perhaps did not agree with a possible solution which the worker has been considering. On the other hand the worker may rejoice that a decision had been made for him without his having to expend mental energy making it himself. The lazy man's answer to problem-solving – have someone else do it for you! The consequences of this attitude are varied.

The decision may turn out to be the wrong one and the worker can take comfort in avoiding responsibility and lay the blame, rightly, on the decision-making manager. If, however, the manager eventually blames the worker, which often happens, a bad relationship can develop. What usually tends to happen, however, is that the decision is acted upon and all is happiness. Unfortunately when another problem arises in which the same worker is involved, the immediate action is to take the problem to the manager because 'the boss sorted things out last time there was a problem, so he'll do it this time!'. As a result, a proportion of the manager's time is taken up with solving other people's problems rather than using management time effectively, and good opportunities for coaching and developing staff have been lost.

The third option recognizes that

- the manager/supervisor is not the only one capable of making a decision
- the manager/supervisor is not the only one who *should* make a decision
- the ownership of a problem lies with the one on whom the problem is having an effect
- problems are opportunities for the development of people involved in the problem.

In order to fulfil these requirements the manager must ensure that, provided it is not his sole responsibility, the person who brings the problem is encouraged to solve it himself. This can be achieved through a counselling process in which the counsellor resists every attempt, either on his own part or that of the other person, to have him solve the problem for the other person. Instead the problem owner is encouraged to consider the solution options himself, to select the most suitable and to make the decision for action. This is a very effective combination of counselling and coaching.

The benefits of this option are that the manager will avoid a drain on his time and will build up a staff who are capable of solving problems and who are less likely to rely on others for decision making. The staff will benefit personally through increased skill, progressive development and an increase in personal capabilities and self-confidence. These developments will aid the individual in career or job progression and will consequently improve job satisfaction.

JOB APPRAISAL REVIEW

The manager can of course initiate interactions with his staff with the intention of developing contact, communication and relationships. One mechanism for furthering this on a relatively formal basis and which is now part of the environment of many organizations, is the job appraisal review which is linked with the formal annual report on individuals. The appraisal review or interview will be dealt with in detail in Chapter 12, but it is so important in employee relationships that a general description at this stage will be worth while.

An annual review procedure within an organization can take many forms. But whatever the nature of the review, the basic intention is to tell/discuss with the individual the extent of the effectiveness of his or her performance during the past year and to look forward to the coming year. The raison d'être of the appraisal interview is based on the many surveys which have been undertaken to determine what employees are looking for from their management. Invariably, high on the list of needs is the giving of feedback on how the worker's performance is seen by more senior management – being told what is expected of one and how one is seen in relation to these expectations.

Unfortunately, many managers regard this annual review as their release from any other contact or feedback opportunities and only talk to their subordinates in this way at the once-a-year event. This is the reason for the many horror stories one hears, when at the interview the interviewee is suddenly confronted with a list of all the things he has done wrong during the year, many of which he was not aware that he had been in error. The appraisal interview should be the culmination of a continuous dialogue between the manager and the worker throughout the year in which praise and blame should have come out at the time. It is not a weapon with which to attack the worker with criticisms which should have emerged earlier. If this negative approach is used, the manager has obviously lost the opportunity to create and maintain a developing relationship. Managers who operate 'kicks and carrots' on a continuing basis are likely to have a more natural staff relationship, which can be further strengthened by the introduction of interim 'mini' appraisal interviews at six-monthly or even three-monthly intervals. These reviews which are much less formal than the annual review, are to check progress and modify plans by introducing more realistic time scales. They may easily be linked with regular reviews of the task progress within the normal planning cycle.

However, contacts with staff are not always as pleasant or as friendly as those described. There will certainly be times when the worker comes with a complaint or the manager has to take disciplinary action against an individual. These occasions fall within the formal interview situations experienced by all managers but, although the two events are quite different in their nature, the philosophy must be common as far as the manager is concerned – the event must be dealt with positively and constructively rather than in an offhand or negative way. The latter attitude will not only destroy the immediate situation, but may invoke the potential future deterioration of relationships. Consequently managers must consciously want to help people and must also be skilled in the techniques and methods of interviewing. Subsequent chapters of the book will address these techniques and methods.

To summarize the ways to develop good staff relationships as well as effective interviewing skills, a manager should talk to his staff/workers/employees

- regularly
- realistically
- meaningfully
- with empathy for all
- giving every opportunity for formal meetings
- honestly, particularly when giving feedback.

Any manager who has the best interests of his staff at heart must be prepared to devote time to one-to-one interactions with them, in other words to accept or initiate some form of interview. It is essential for the effective manager to conduct the best interview possible. The skills of interviewing, although extensive, are not impossible to learn and a skilled interviewer can make all the difference between an enjoyable and a distressing experience for both participants. These skills which are described in the following chapters will ease the paths, whatever the nature of the interview.

2 The basics of interviewing

Everybody at some time in their lives, mostly on more than one occasion, experiences what is known as being interviewed. Many have the reverse experience of being the interviewer. It may sound a simple question, but our starting point must be, on whichever side we are, what is this event we call an *interview*? How do we distinguish it from other interactions with people? Once I thought that this was a simple question for which there should be a simple answer, until I tried to find it!

Various definitions can be examined and rejected for different reasons: perhaps there is no simple definition, rather a set of circumstances which add up to what we call an interview. The circumstances comprise

- two or more people
- meeting in a formal or semi-formal situation
- where there is a specific purpose for meeting which is known to all concerned
- a structure is followed
- one or more persons take the controlling (interviewer) role, the other or others taking the more responsive (interviewee) role
- usually seated, although not always
- usually pre-planned, though not always, preferably by both sides
- awareness by both sides that an interview is taking place and acceptance that one is the interviewer, the other the interviewee.

This is not the tidy type of description we expect, but it includes most of the criteria that distinguish an interview from a conversation, discussion or a group meeting, even when the group consists of only two people.

We are on safer ground when we consider the occasions on which an interview can occur. These may include

- an employment selection
- an employment selection panel
- a promotion panel
- a job appraisal review
- a reprimand or disciplinary hearing
- a grievance
- an information-seeking interview (including, for example, an interview under caution)
- an opinion-finding interview such as might be found in street or door-to-door research
- a counselling interview
- an employment termination
- a planning interview.

Many of these types of interview have common parts, but it is often the combination, inclusion or exclusion of the various parts which creates the difference. A disciplinary interview often includes

- an information/opinion seeking section
- a reprimand section
- a counselling section which looks at remedial action.

An interview of this nature if approached in the rather heavy-handed manner of some years ago or of the present-day autocrat, would include only one element – the reprimand.

One of the principal elements in considering the different types of interview is the underlying structure. But other factors combine with the structure to give a particular interview its specific form and identity. These will include

- the physical aspects
- the questioning techniques
- the level of questioning

- the interview behaviours.

PHYSICAL ASPECTS

Many of the physical or administrative aspects of the interview appear to be simply so much common sense that it hardly seems worth reminding readers of them, even those with little experience of interviewing. But common sense can let us down and in the heat of the moment the most obviously necessary things can be forgotten.

Privacy

If the maximum benefit is to be obtained from an interview, it must be held in an environment where the participants can interact without being overheard or observed. Consequently the maximum amount of privacy must be obtained. In most cases the privacy of sound is considered naturally, but often the equal need for privacy of sight is ignored. For example, an occasion may arise during the interview when the interviewee may want to cry. This cathartic release may not occur if the event could be observed by others and consequently the objective of the interview may not be achieved.

Privacy for its own sake is obviously necessary. Few of us would open up as we would do in a private interview if we had to talk in front of a number of other people. If this facility is not provided all that is likely to emerge is the superficial comment which may not represent the problem at all. The private environment affords opportunity at least for interviewees to open up as far as they wish to do. There can be problems in providing the necessary privacy. Many commercial work areas, for example, are now on the open-plan system; interviewers may have to share rooms with others; or there may be noisy environs. But these are no insoluble problems and it is usually possible to find somewhere which offers at least some elements of privacy. In very favourable situations, special rooms are set aside in the organization for interviews or other private occasions. On the other hand a quiet corner in the canteen when it is not being used for its normal purposes could be suitable. Perhaps the location may not be ideal, but there is usually the opportunity for something better than public space, and this *must* be sought.

There are, however, difficulties in setting up an interview in a 'different' place, even if privacy is impossible in the interviewer's room. If the interview is of a helping nature, both the interviewer and interviewee must be as relaxed as possible as early as possible. In a strange room the pressure of the situation is exacerbated for both and will obviously have an effect on the atmosphere of the interview, at least in the important early stages. The interviewee may be suspicious if the interviewer suggests going elsewhere than his room for the interview.

The telephone, that most pervasive element of modern life, must certainly not be allowed to intrude in an interview. It would seem the most obvious action to stop telephone interventions while an interview is taking place, but it is one item which is forgotten more than any other – an obvious sign of the times that we take the telephone so much for granted. There can be few things worse in an interview than to reach a critical stage of the interaction only to have the whole mood destroyed by the interruption of a telephone call. It has to be answered, however curtly, which might take a shorter or longer time depending on whether the caller is the boss, a peer, a subordinate, a client or a personal caller. Its effect on the progress of the interview may take some time to repair, if ever. The interviewee may feel, particularly if the meeting has been arranged for some time, that the interviewer considers it of so little importance that he has taken no special steps to help the process.

Most telephone systems are capable of circumventing incoming calls either by a complete stop being put upon them or by re-routing them to another extension. This can be done either by a switchboard operator or by a computerized system. Internal calls can be a problem when a switchboard operator takes incoming calls only. If all else fails, disengage the receiver.

Similar efforts must be made to avoid more direct interruptions – another person bursting into the room during the interview or, even more annoying, a persistent knocking at the door. If there is no external guardian, place an 'Engaged – do not enter' sign on the door, if this piece of apparatus is not an integral part of the door. Again it is so easy to forget this and suffer the interrruption.

Seating

There must be some form of seating for all involved parties and even this simple item of furniture can become an (over) important aspect of the interview.

It used to be common practice for interviewers to place themselves in a more powerful position than those they were interviewing, often even by having a higher chair. I knew one manager, and have had the same fact reported to me by colleagues about other managers, who placed blocks under his chair legs to bring them to a higher level. I hope these days have gone.

There has been a lot of research into the significance of the seating position in interviews or other two-person interactions. Experience generally supports this, but it must be applied carefully and not just because such and such a researcher has stated that this is the best method.

There are three principal seating positions for the interviewee in relation to the interviewer, although they are only indications, not absolute positions. It is simpler to refer to these positions in relation to a table, although this actual physical presence is not necessary. The positions are shown in Figure 2.1 as x, y and z in descending order of formality.

Position x is more or less opposite the interviewer and this is the classic 'across the table' position of confrontation. The table acts as a physical and mental barrier, introducing distance between the two parties, and the attitude between the parties becomes more formal and structured. If the interviewer places the interviewee in this position, or if the

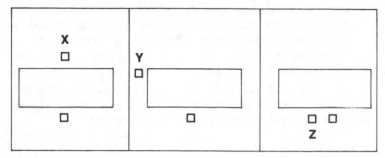

Figure 2.1   Seating position of interviewee in relation to interviewer

interviewee voluntarily chooses the position, the one is telling the other that they want the interview to be conducted in that manner.

Position z represents the other extreme where the interactive relationships are more likely to be informal and friendly. A parallel can be drawn with the non-interview situation of two friends, particularly where an established sexual relationship has developed – the two friends are more likely to sit side by side than in any other position. In a more official, work-related context, this position might occur in a coaching event with the mentor and student sitting side by side in a helping, friendly configuration.

The compromise between x and z is of course the diagonal midway position at y. Here both parties are willing to move away from the frontal 'attack' position, but the relationship is not quite sufficiently advanced or relevant for the very informal positions. Position y can in many cases be considered to be the 'normal', at work seating position when the seat 'owner' wants a reasonably easy relationship with his clients.

These seating arrangements can of course work in both directions. The way in which the interviewer positions the seats can be taken as a non-verbal signal to the interviewee that the relationship of the interaction is intended to be in a particular mode – x, y or z. Of course, this intention can be completely upset by the interviewee. If, for example, the chair is in the halfway y position and the interviewee feels that he wants to keep the interviewer at arm's length, he may move the chair to the x position. The interviewer will see the move and realize its significance.

In some cases it is useful to identify the attitude of the incoming interviewee. I have tried this by having the only other chair placed well away from the desk and inviting the interviewee to 'pull up a chair'. Where the chair is placed can indicate the interviewee's frame of mind.

However, one has to be very careful in the interpretation of signals of this nature. People may be conditioned in a particular way which may affect their behaviour. For example, an office I once occupied was cleaned each evening by different cleaners and I always knew when it had been done by a particular person. My 'other' chair was kept in the y position, but whenever this cleaner was on duty, the following morning when I entered the room I always found the chair placed firmly and squarely directly opposite mine. My interpretation of this was that if this cleaner had to be interviewed she would only feel comfortable with the chair in position x. One evening I was working late and this cleaner came in. I asked her to sit down and wait as I would only be a few minutes. She did so, by moving the chair from y to x! I asked her why she had done this and she replied that this was the position a chair had to be in when at a desk. Any interview for employment she had attended, the chair had always been in that position.

Many managers who attend an interview training course usually learn about the seating research and decide to take action on their return to work. Consequently, their 'other' chair is moved to y, the safe friendly position. In some cases, the manager's style of leadership may have been autocratic or tending in that direction and the subordinates will have come to expect the chair to be in its usual formal, x, position. When they see it is not where they expected it to be, a typical reaction might be one of suspicion rather than acceptance that a less formal overture has been attempted. Perhaps in such cases a gradual movement of the chair from x and y may be sufficient to allay suspicion, particularly if the other aspects of the leadership style are also modified.

The safest approach might be to allow the interviewee to place the chair where they wish. They will most likely put it where they feel most comfortable. Unless of course it is the specific intention of the interviewer to control the interview from the entrance.

Other arrangements. One other consideration to be taken into account when arranging the seating is to avoid 'third degree' lighting – direct glare, usually sunlight, into the interviewee's eyes. The interviewer may only become aware of it (if at all) during the interview when it is noticed that the interviewee is sitting with screwed-up eyes against the glare. Such a position cannot be comfortable, otherwise sunglasses would not have been invented. You can usually avoid this simply by a small movement of the chair before the interview. The interviewee may not wish to take that action himself because of pressure already existing with the interview. Do not assume on this and other aspects that interviewees would take any action to alleviate discomfort they might be suffering.

Whatever physical or other arrangements of an administrative nature are necessary, remember to give some forethought to these aspects before the interview. Consideration of this nature is an integral part of the planning process, to which we shall return on more than one occasion.

3 Viewpoints, structure and questioning

Not all processes rely on a strictly mechanical progression to achieve success: this is certainly the case with interviewing. A bottling plant *must* follow a strict sequence of operations if a full, stoppered bottle with a correctly placed label is to emerge at the end of the process line. But when we are considering an interview, we are taking into account that people do not behave in the same way as inanimate machinery. Consequently there are no golden rules or standard methods of approaching any one type of interview. However, practice and experience, often supported or suggested by psychological research, suggests that an interaction is more likely to succeed if it progresses in a more or less logical manner. Even so, there must be no slavish concentration on the logical path, rather the interviewer must be prepared, and able, to deviate if the situation demands.

The level of skill of an interviewer is relevant here. If we ignore the minority of people who are 'natural' interviewers and need no training, a potential interviewer can start with a high probability of falling into the traps of side-issues, red herrings, confusion and omission of essentials which pervade most interviews. The trained, skilled, experienced interviewer can follow the planned path, but can immediately react to and cope with anything which might arise, knowing that he can take up the natural interview course when the unexpected has been dealt with. The best advice to the newcomer is to learn the structures, techniques and methods of interviewing and to follow these paths in the early interview. Deviation should only be allowed when a lead introduced as a very important aspect to the interviewee is not taken up. As experience increases, and the interviewer becomes skilled in assessing the person to be interviewed, tunes can be played on the structure and/ or techniques, even to the extent of turning them on their heads. But this must be attempted only with extreme caution. It is dangerous to play games with people, purely for the sake of it. An interviewer has to know not only the extent of his own skills as an interviewer, but also the skill and acceptance level of the interviewee. Remember that the interviewee has feelings and reactions. There is little value in conducting a 'loose' interview when the interviewee wants a tightly structured, formal interview so that he knows exactly where he is.

VIEWPOINTS

The same interview may be approached in different ways according to the viewpoint of various individuals. Imagine a group of people standing at the summit of a mountain and looking down to the valleys below. The individuals in that group will be having different thoughts about what they see, depending on their viewpoints of life and these viewpoints can be identified from their physical and verbal reactions.

Figure 3.1 suggests the internal dialogues of the observers, representing the various viewpoints which can be taken. For example, B who thinks 'looking all the way round and down, isn't it all wonderful', is taking a global view and in other situations may be uncomfortable if forced to look at specifics too soon. An interview with this type may need a long introductory period before settling down to the main point. However, if that approach is used with A who has 'reached the top of the mountain and immediately wants to do something else', it may result in failure. In such a case, 'Good morning. Let's get down to business' may be more effective. This is perhaps the most difficult aspect of interviewing. If the interviewer does not know the

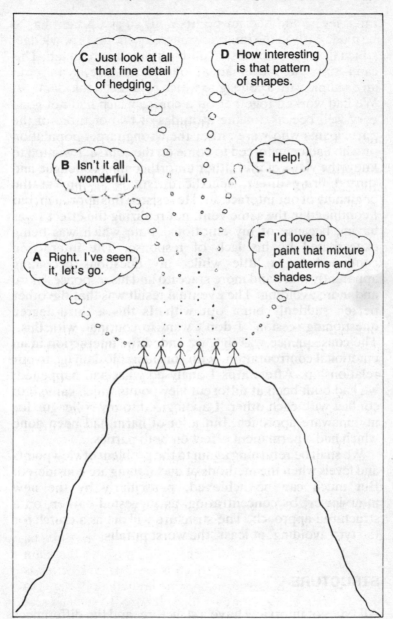

Figure 3.1   Viewpoints

interviewee and his viewpoints well, an assessment has to be made early in the interview based on limited knowledge, which then has to be tested and continued or rejected. This can result in an inordinate amount of damage. I can recall an example with a colleague which resulted in this damage. We had worked together on a course which had not gone very well because of the attitudes of two or three of the participants who were either the wrong target population or who had been forced to come on the course. I wanted to know the views of this rather unforthcoming colleague and started firing direct, specific questions at him at the beginning of our interaction. He resisted this approach, but I continued in the same vein, not realizing the effect I was having because of my emotional state which was being exacerbated by his lack of response. The interaction continued for a little while, my questions becoming apparently more and more staccato and his responses more and more avoiding. The eventual result was that the other person suddenly burst out with 'Is this a third-degree questioning session? I don't want to continue with this.' The consequence was that we ended the interaction in an emotional confrontation, with considerable damage to our relationship. Afterwards I analysed what had happened; we had both been at different viewpoints which came into conflict with each other. I apologized to my colleague for my unaware approach, but a lot of harm had been done which had a permanent effect on both parties.

We shall be returning again to the problem of viewpoints and levels when the methods of questioning are considered. But much can be achieved, particularly by the new interviewer, by concentrating, as suggested earlier, on a structured approach. The structure will act as a crutch for the tyro avoiding, at least, the worst pitfalls.

STRUCTURE

All types of interview have a structure, and the differences between types are reflected in the various structures – some merely minor variations. We shall, therefore, make only minor comment on some of the interviews because of these small variations.

It was suggested earlier (see Chapter 2) that the principal types of interview include

- employment selection
- employment selection panel
- promotion panel
- job appraisal
- reprimand or disciplinary action
- grievances
- information seeking
- opinion finding
- counselling
- termination
- planning
- coaching
- training

Some of these types of interview are more common to managers and supervisors than others, and the remainder, in addition to others not listed, are often simple variations. The more common ones will again vary from one manager or supervisor to another. From my own experience the most common have been

- planning
- promotion panel
- job appraisal
- counselling
- discipline
- coaching, and
- training.

The discipline interview has been included in this second listing because, although not necessarily common in numerical terms, most managers and supervisors find it so difficult that it is usually quoted whenever interviews are discussed.

Decisions

Some interviews, for example discipline and job appraisal, are under the effective control of the interviewer before the interaction starts – they are initiated by the interviewer. As even the occurrence of the interview is in the hands of the interviewer, most of the parameters for the interaction can be set by that person – the time, place and even the mood. This is determined beforehand because the interviewer has time to consider any necessary planning. Some will obviously require more planning than others, for example the discipline interview where the interviewer will have to be sure of his ground before proceeding and will also have to plan the reprimand to avoid unecessary repercussions.

In some cases time will not allow for sufficient pre-interview planning and the interviewer may be able to delay its timing. However, there are occasions when the interviewer will have no prior knowledge of the problem and its seriousness, and will have to commence the interview without any warning. In such cases the time allocated to the interview may also not be subject to any pre-planned constraints.

The interviews just described can certainly be of the grievance or counselling natures. One person with a grievance may request an immediate interview and another may announce that they have a problem and would like an (immediate) interview (of a counselling nature). The words in parentheses are usually not spoken. In both instances the interviewer has three options:

- to refuse the interview altogether: an unwise move in any circumstance
- to accept immediately the interview request
- to suggest a delay to a more convenient time.

If the interview is accepted immediately, the interviewer obviously has no opportunity for planning or preparation, although if the problem was not known beforehand no planning would have been possible. In such circumstances the interviewer must be prepared to react to virtually anything which might be presented to him, and also to cancel or suspend other actions which may or may not be important.

On the other hand, delay of the interview with the agreement of the interviewee will allow the interviewer (a) to prepare himself for the event and plan, at least, the approach, and (b) to try to find out by other means what the problem may be, so that he can plan some moves in relation to the content of the problem. The simplest way, of course, if a delay is agreed, is to ask the person requesting the interview to state briefly the nature of the problem and its urgency. The principal danger here is that the requester may immediately launch into the problem.

The interviewer must ensure there is no unavoidable delay especially if it is apparent that this would place additional distress on the person requesting the interview. Where an immediate attempt is made to determine the nature of the problem, the interviewer must not only listen to the words but must also weigh the verbal response against other possible visible signs of stress – unusual nervous actions, a higher pitch of the voice, exaggerated hand movements, faster speech, etc. Unfortunately for the interviewer, some people are capable of hiding these normal signs of stress. Consequently the observed non-verbal signals may be out of step with the verbal statements, resulting in misinterpretation of the urgency of the request.

A manager must decide on his philosophy towards counselling required by his staff. Two main reasons for counselling exist – work-related problems and external, personal problems. The manager cannot escape from his responsibilities in work-related problems and must take some form of action. However, with personal problems he must decide whether to become involved in any way. Decisions of this nature are very difficult because non-work-related problems can so easily become work-related and hence the direct responsibility of the manager. Much of this decision making will revolve around the leadership style of the manager and the manager-subordinate relationships.

There is much less, if any, latitude allowed to the

manager in cases where grievances are involved. Where grievances emerge at work they are usually related to work and thus become the responsibility of the manager. Other considerations occur with the conduct of the grievance interview – high emotion, involvement of the manager, accompanied interviewees etc. These will be discussed later.

The structures for other types of interview will be considered later when specific interviews are being discussed.

QUESTIONING

Although interviews are based mainly on questioning by the interviewer, it is more effective to create an atmosphere in which the interviewee is encouraged not only to give answers but also to raise questions. Consequently the method of questioning can have a considerable impact on the success or at least the smooth running of the interview. However, one important point must be emphasized. A successful interview, or at least the investigative part, depends on the emergence of all the necessary information. This may not result necessarily from skilled and appropriate questioning techniques: the interviewee may want to air the problem in which case the information will emerge whatever the interviewer might do! For example, in most grievance interviews the interviewer only needs to be there for the complaint to come pouring out.

However, in the same way that the newcomer to interviewing was advised to follow a structure, at least in his early events, so with questioning. Poor questioning technique can upset an interviewee to such an extent that little success results from the event. Equally, good interviewing methods will not always produce all the required information. But there is a greater likelihood of success if an appropriate method is used – after all every interviewer of whatever skill level needs as much as possible going for him if the interview is to be successful. So in the early stages of skill acquisition, the interviewer is advised to stick to the form of questioning which has been shown, from observation of many interviews, to work.

As we have seen, the role of the interviewer at least in the investigatory stages of an interview, is that of questioner, whether for the purpose of selection, discipline, guidance, grievance etc. The purpose of the questions will depend on the situation either of the interview or of the stage of the interview. They may be to elicit information, ideas, opinions, thoughts, views, feelings or, having obtained these, to probe for hidden or undisclosed meanings, additional information or clarification, or to test understanding or check agreement. Whatever the reason, the questioning must be effective and ensure that what is sought is in fact elicited.

Many interview training courses stress the importance of the questioning technique, which the newcomer is well-advised to follow. But other than in the case of the newcomer, slavish devotion to technique can sometimes be ineffective. The interviewer must be aware of the *effect* of the questioning and the information which is or is not being obtained, and be prepared to be flexible in the approach. My own experience with countless interviews has been that very few cases, for example, the 'bad' closed type of question, have produced only the bare answer 'yes/no', unless that was the only possible answer. There are of course occasions when a closed question will invite a closed answer and the interviewer will have to ask further questions to obtain the necessary information.

However, most people unless they are

- very aggressive or defensive
- very awkward, whether deliberately or not, or
- very inarticulate

are likely to say 'yes/no' and then go on voluntarily to give a fuller answer which supplements the simple initial response. The two types of attitude – aggressiveness/ defensiveness and awkwardness – are more likely to be found in the discipline interview than in most other interactions, so in these situations it is obviously to the interviewer's benefit to avoid this problem by using more appropriate techniques.

Even the experienced interviewer can come to grief. I can recall when I was visiting schools giving career guidance interviews to school-leavers, a task in which I related well to this group of people and usually managed to get them to open up quite easily. On one occasion I was warned that I was unlikely to obtain anything from one particular boy. I'm afraid that my ego must have been riding rather high at that time as I was convinced that by using open questions and silence, I would be successful where others had failed. I began with an 'open' invitation: 'Tell me what sort of jobs you have thought you might like'. The response was a deafening silence. After a while I said 'Well, you may not have had any ideas yet so tell me what you like doing most at school'. I was determined to withstand the ensuing silence, but it continued for so long that I was the first to break. I decided to use a more direct, closed approach. 'Do you like sports?' received exactly the same treatment and I had to admit defeat. The only consolation I received was given by the teacher who had pre-warned me: I was congratulated on the fact that he hadn't run away as usually happened when even relative strangers spoke to him!

Both 'closed' and 'open' questioning terminology has already been used here. Let us consider these and other questioning techniques in common use.

Closed questions

These are questions which would normally attract the basic answer 'yes/no' or would elicit a statement of fact which was strictly limited. For example:

- 'Have you a current driving licence?' Response: 'Yes I have' or 'No I haven't'
- 'When were you born?' Response: '(the date of birth)'.

Of course, if the respondant is feeling helpful and does not want to contain the answer simply within what was asked, the responses might be:

- 'Yes I have, but it expires in two weeks so I shall have to remember to renew it'
- '(date of birth). I don't know whether you believe in astrology but that makes me a Gemini.'

In general, however, a question receives the response it deserves and the questioner should be prepared to receive a closed answer to a closed question. The intention may have been simply to obtain the specific factual information and if more information is given this may disturb the *questioner* who sought only a particular response.

Closed questions may also be used deliberately to control an interview in a particular way. It may be that the interviewee does not need to be encouraged to talk and therefore any approach which uses questions designed to attract articulation is superfluous and inappropriate. Even more so, the interviewee may be too keen on talking and the interviewer may wish to restrict his answers rather than extend them. One method of doing this is to ask deliberately closed questions, preferably those to which the answer 'yes/no' only can be given, or in the other type of closed question, a simple statement of information will be the response. This approach, if the interviewer perseveres, will work except with the most insistent talker.

However, the interviewer must not become too locked in on an insistence to ask other than closed questions. They are quite common in ordinary conversation and have their place there and during interviews. As suggested earlier, most people, unless they are in a certain behavioural state, will give more than just a simple answer. But even the most articulate respondant will become weary of an inept interviewer using too many closed questions without this deliberate intention.

Multiple questions

These can cause more problems to the interviewee than closed ones because they are more likely to confuse. For example:

- 'Now I should like you to tell me what you felt about that particular job, but before that could you tell me how you obtained the job, and I should also like to know why you felt you should move on from there?'

The interviewee (or anyone else) would be thoroughly confused. He is being asked to describe first a feeling, then more of a fact, then another feeling completely different from the areas of the other two questions. Consequently he will not know how to respond, at what level, and to which question – if indeed they have all been identified, and remembered.

Memory is the first problem. When an interviewee is being asked a question he will normally concentrate on the parts or even words of the question. In the above case, the concentration would naturally be on the first part of the question and answer would start to be formulated in the interviewee's mind. But as the second part forms a second question which will require similar concentration, the earlier parts are at risk of being forgotten or even being twisted. A similar reaction will occur when the interviewer continues with yet another question in the third part.

The result of this attack on the interviewee's powers of retention in what might already be a traumatic event, might be complete confusion, or as is often the case, retention of the final question only or even part of the final question. In consequence, it is this part of the overall question which will be answered. This could cause some frustration in the mind of the interviewer who cannot understand why the interviewee 'cannot answer the question I asked him'.

If the range of questions is identified and remembered, the interviewee is still in trouble. Which question should he answer? Should he try to answer all the questions? In which order should he try to answer? In other words, confusion is again present in the interviewee's mind and this will almost certainly be exhibited in the response, to his detriment in the interviewer's opinion of him. Either this confused response attempt to answer all parts will result; or the last part only of the question will come through, identified by the interviewee as what the interviewer really wanted; or the interviewee will answer the part that he *wants* to answer, the part which is easiest to answer or presents the least risk.

This will cause difficulties for the interviewer. It may be that he wanted and expected answers to all parts of the question, or the part which was answered was not the priority in the questioner's mind. Consequently the interviewer has to decide on a reaction to the response and will have to think up other questions to obtain the desired information.

Sometimes the multiple question will be of value. It may be necessary to probe the interviewee's depth of understanding and skill at dealing with problem situations. If the interviewee can retain a number of different questions and answer them fully, rationally and logically, this will demonstrate a likely capability of coping well with complex situations. Of course, the most obvious way of dealing with a multiple question is to ask the questioner which question he wishes to have answered. However, an interviewee can only do this if he is very sure of his ground and will not suffer as a result of what is a challenge to the interviewer.

Multiple choice questions

A less threatening and more appropriate form of the multiple question is the multiple choice question. Here the interviewee is given a relatively simple choice between two or more options. Such a question might be: 'When you saw the car coming towards you, did you have any sort of mental blackout or did various choices flash through your mind?'. There is obviously a strong element of learning in a question of this nature in that the interviewee has the opportunity of at least having an answer (always assuming that all the possible choices were known by the questioner). It can also introduce an element of pressure into the situation. The interviewee is forced into the position of almost *having* to make the choice.

This type of pressure questioning is quite common in some sales and negotiation interactions in order to ensure a

positive answer from the other person. Pressure is
obviously being placed on the customer when he is asked,
'Which colour would you prefer, red or blue?' as opposed
to the more open question 'Which colour would you
prefer?'. In the second case the resultant possibility is that a
choice might be made which is not a preferred one in the
sales approach and might in fact result in a loss of sale.

Leading questions

'Don't you think it would be best if . . .?' is usually
recognized as an inappropriate form of questioning. In such
a case the answer is being put into the respondant's mouth
and the desired response will be given particularly if the
interviewee is under pressure – even though it may not be
the answer the interviewee wants to give.

Under normal circumstances this leading would not be
desirable, but, as with all other forms of questioning so far
discussed, there may be occasions when it might be
desirable or necessary and therefore justified. The deliberate use of this question may be to let the interviewee
know the line of response or attitude the interviewer is
seeking. Consequently the interviewee is given the
opportunity to decide whether or not he can accept this
line. Alternatively, it can be used effectively to test
whether the interviewee has opinions of his own which he is
willing to express and which apparently run contrary to the
views of the interviewer. The latter approach may be used,
albeit deviously, to sort out existing or potential 'yes-men'.

Non-questions

The most difficult question with which the interviewee may
have to deal is the non-question. The interviewer presents
the question in such a way that the interviewee either
doesn't understand it or may not even realize that a
question has been asked. I once appeared before an
internal selection panel on which one of the three

interviewers was well known for his long-windedness in conversation and discussion. When his turn to question me came round he started talking and continued for at least three minutes. During this period several questions were raised and I was on the point of responding when the interviewer answered them himself and carried on talking. Eventually he stopped talking, but without, as far as I could identify, asking me a question. I had to apologize and ask what was the question being posed! Fortunately the chairman of the panel then intervened and said that he too was interested in what question was being asked.

Open questions

The most positive and usually most productive form of questioning is known as the open question technique. As the name suggests, the question is framed in such a way that the respondant is given the opportunity to expand in his response and give a full and open answer. The question 'In which types of spare-time activities are you interested?' is sufficiently specific to let the respondant know the type of information required, yet allows him room in which to answer as widely as he may wish. The response to the above question, if the respondant has a wide range of interests, could be long and complex and could require a number of supplementary questions to bring out the full information, if that is what the interviewer requires.

From the description of the other types of questions it will be seen that the responses of the interviewee can be manipulated to some extent by the form of the question. The type of manipulation will depend on the objectives of the interviewer and, if he is reasonably skilled, it will in general result in the desired response. But equally he must be prepared for this response and be ready to act accordingly. In the case, for example, of closed questions, the response will probably be closed and consequently the interviewer must be ready to ask another question or take some other action. The response to an open question must logically be looked for as an open answer with plenty of information being given or feelings, views or opinions being expressed. This type of response demands that the questioner be prepared to listen, and to listen carefully. In a full response a number of statements might be made, some almost as asides, but which could cover important or significant views. If the interviewer really wants to extract the maximum value from the interview and the specific open question, he must be constantly on the lookout for these verbal clues, and store them for retrieval when the interviewee completes his contribution. Reference back is essential, otherwise, apart from significant information being lost, the interviewee may feel that if something he has said is not taken up – and he may have slipped it in with this intention – the interviewer has not been listening to him. If you do not want an open answer, do not ask an open question!

Not every open question will be treated to a full and open answer. The reasons for a more controlled response can be many, ranging from inarticulateness to a determined attitude not to disclose too much. A closed response when an open one is desired can be very restricting and many interviewers might turn away and admit defeat. But, unless it is apparent that the lack of response is due to an uncooperative attitude, it may be that the interviewee requires some encouragement to talk. This will mean continued effort on the part of the interviewer, perhaps with further open questions, perhaps with other techniques. Rarely will reversion to closed questioning be of help since this will result only in a compounding of the brief, unhelpful responses.

Many interviewers find it difficult to phrase open questions because they have to be constructed more carefully than closed questions. The technique which I have found always works for me is to preface the question with Kipling's 'honest serving men' – how, what, where, when, why and who. There is no guarantee that the required response will result, but the likelihood becomes greater. Questions using these prefaces could take the form of:

- *How* did you achieve these results?
- *What* kind of aircraft have you piloted?
- *Why* did that incident occur?
- *When* will it be necessary to leave?
- *Who* will have the responsibility at the different stages?
- *Where* will we find out about the new arrangements?

Some of the preface words will have a more open connotation than others and the nature of the question will influence the openness of the response. For example, the response to 'What kind of aircraft have you piloted?' could be the simple, one word 'Cessna'. However, 'What kind of feelings did you have at that stage?' is more likely to produce an extensive and meaningful response.

Testing understanding

The final form of positive questioning to be considered introduces wider aspects of the techniques. It is known as testing understanding or checking out. Too often in our interactions with others we assume, incorrectly, that they have understood what we have said or equally, that we have understood what they have said.

If the interviewee makes a statement or proposal, or a series of complex statements or proposals, the interviewer might say: 'If I have understood you correctly, you are saying (suggesting) . . . . Have I got that right?' This type of approach has a number of valuable uses:

- It gives the interviewer the chance to check out his/her understanding of what has been said
- It gives the interviewee the opportunity to correct any misunderstandings on the part of the interviewer
- It informs the interviewee that he/she has said what was intended to be said
- It demonstrates that listening has taken place
- If more than two people are present at the interaction, it summarizes and clarifies the interviewee's contribution, for the benefit of the other people.

Checking out can also be used in the reverse direction, with the interviewer ensuring that the interviewee has understood what the interviewer has said. The obvious way to do this is to ask the other person if he has understood what has been said. However the answer 'yes' might be untrue in order that the interviewee does not lose face in his own eyes by admitting an apparent weakness. Similarly, adverse reactions might result from being too direct and asking the other to repeat what has been said. Most people find it useful to say something like: 'So that I can check out that I said what I meant to say, would you care to summarize what you heard.'

This invitation is subtly different from asking the other simply to repeat the material. It throws the emphasis on the interviewer rather than on any possible failings of the interviewee.

A question in an interview is therefore not just a question; there is much more to it. Interviewers must be careful not only in what they say, but how it is said and with what obvious or apparent intentions. A further support for the philosophy of planning and structuring the interview, rather than just allowing it to happen.

4 Analysing behaviour

Although questioning is an important part of an interview, some of the other possible behaviours may be equally important in making the interview real and effective.

INVITING

One of the behaviours which is difficult to classify can be labelled inviting. This is a mixture between proposing and asking a question. It is probably more allied to the open question and the desired response in terms of length and depth can be similar. Very few people, apart from the different characters cited in Chapter 3, can resist an invitation couched in terms of: 'Tell me all about the places you have visited'. This may appear in written form to be a hard proposal or almost an order, but when expressed in a particular tone of voice or with certain intonations, it will be obvious as an open and friendly invitation.

This appearance of being an order can be removed by a further change of word which, although having the appearance of a question, is still basically an invitation: 'Would you like/care to tell me about these problems you have?'

If these invitations are accepted, which is most likely, the flood gates could open and the inviter, perhaps even more than the straightforward questioner, must be prepared for this. Having opened these gates he must really listen to what emerges from this flood of information, feelings, views and opinions, some of which may be irrelevant. The inviter would be unwise to stem the flood, however irrelevant it may seem – after all, it has resulted from his invitation.

REFLECTING

Although having similarities with questioning, reflecting stands in its own right as a powerful interviewing behaviour. However, it can backfire to an even greater extent than the most inept questioning. In this technique the interviewer restates or reflects, briefly, what the interviewee has just said perhaps incompletely. The reflection obviates the need for the interviewer to think of a question to ask in order to obtain more information, a question which may not produce the desired response. An interviewee who may be having some difficulty in expressing what he wants to say, may make a contribution such as: 'There seems to be something not quite right in the office'. If the next contribution by the interviewer is 'What is wrong?' the interviewee's response could easily be 'I'm not quite sure.'

This will make the interviewer probe more deeply to obtain what he feels is still submerged, a probing which the interviewee might shy away from or directly reject.

The reflective alternative may be, spoken as a neutral statement rather than as a question: 'You may feel there is something not quite right'. This approach, simply reflecting the interviewee's thoughts but which have been left unsaid, acts as a continuation of these thoughts and encourages the interviewee, in effect, to let the thoughts surface verbally. The response may then be something like: 'Hmmmm, yes. One of the things I have seen happening . . .'

As suggested earlier, reflecting behaviour has to be used with care and the interviewer has to be aware all the time of the effect it may be having. If the interviewee sees the reflection for what it is, there may be the danger that the thought will emerge 'He's only saying what I've just told him. What's he up to?' and the interviewee may close up even more.

However, there are two aspects working in the interviewer's favour:

- In most cases the interviewee does want to talk and will welcome any assistance in encouraging this to happen, even if the technique is recognized
- In many cases, particularly those of problem counselling, the interviewee is so engrossed in the emotions of the problem that there is little realization of what the interviewer is doing or saying.

In order to circumvent possible problems arising from the obvious use of reflecting, it is helpful to follow certain rules.

1 Reflect feelings or thoughts only, not facts. A statement that 'I feel there is something I can do about it' suggests a reflective response which will help the speaker to extend the feeling. However, a reflection following the complete statement 'It is 3.30' will be received by the unspoken thought 'What's wrong with him, I've just said that!'

2 Restate the initial contribution using either the same words or other words with the same meaning. This indicates that one does not interpret what has been said, as misinterpretation can so easily occur. If this happens the interaction may be disturbed. It is often more effective to vary the words in some reflections rather than always use the speaker's words. By doing this, the likelihood of reflections being recognized as such will be lessened.

3 Preface the reflection. Useful prefaces are: 'You feel that . . .', 'It seems to you that . . .', 'As you see it . . .', 'What you seem to be saying is . . .' etc. Reflections which use a few of the interviewee's words alone can sound stark and sometimes threatening – 'Something not quite right' can appear to be a challenge to the person's views rather than an encouragement to talk.

4 In general, reflect the last part of what the person has

been saying, ignoring the superfluous, meaningless words or phrases with which we often let our contributions fade away, particularly when we are not sure what we want to say. Usually the last specific but incomplete thing that someone has said is the thought that is in their mind and they are probably still thinking about it.

Reflecting is a helpful behaviour when talking to people whose thoughts on a subject are not completely formed as the part statements being reflected can help them to articulate any extensions of these thoughts. It can also help those people who have articulation problems in any case. A direct question may frighten them and make it more difficult for them to say anything. On the other hand, a reflection, because it is simply saying what they have said, will be seen in a sympathetic light.

The final advantage of this technique is one for the interviewer. Sometimes the interviewer's mind may go blank in the middle of an interview and the immediate reaction is 'What *question* should I ask now? I can't think of one!' A way out of the dilemma may be to reflect part of the previous contribution by the interviewee. This will not only encourage him to talk, with the chance that something significant may emerge, but it will gain some breathing time for the interviewer.

GIVING

One behaviour which is normally regarded in most interviews as the more frequent contribution of the interviewee rather than of the interviewer is *giving* information, feelings, views and opinions. After all, the receipt of these statements is the main purpose of the interview and only following this giving can any more positive action occur. I have said 'rather than of the interview*er*': unfortunately many interviewers use the interview as a platform from which to state their own views and the poor interviewee has to sit there quietly and be subjected to this flow of irrelevant and inappropriate words. All interviewers should remember the golden rule: Ask – then be quiet and listen.

It will sometimes be necessary for the interviewer to give some information: when these instances arise and the need to give is demanded, this must be done. Remember Shakespeare's advice: 'If it were done when 'tis done, then 'twere well it were done quickly'. At the start of the interview the interviewer should tell the interviewee in concise terms the reason for the interview; from then onwards the interviewee must be the major contributor. From time to time the interviewee will pose questions, which must be answered accurately, fully and concisely. The emphasis will usually be on contributions by the interviewee. When possible solutions or methods are being considered, the interviewer will probably need to suggest some approaches – once more, concisely – then over again to the interviewee for him to consider them.

An example of the giving behaviour on the part of the interviewer is summarizing. If the interview is long and complex, rather than relying on the round-up summary at the end of the interview, interim summaries are valuable reminders of what has happened and been agreed to at each stage. But the most important and useful summary must always be the final one to ensure that

- the interviewer knows he has covered everything which he wanted to cover
- the interviewee is satisfied in the same respects
- both the interviewer and interviewee are clear about what has been agreed, who is to do what, and within what time scale
- the opportunity for correction of errors is afforded.

The summarizer must always be careful that the summary is used for the intended purposes. It has been known for the summary – usually a long rambling one – to include aspects which have not been agreed, in order to insert the summarizer's own ideas without doing so in the correct manner. If the other person is not listening intently, these 'inserted' ideas could easily become part of an agreement without the interviewee being aware of what has happened. The greatest danger of this occurring is when the summary is given at the end of the interview and there is also a sense of urgency to complete the interview on time. Under such conditions, particularly if it is the interviewee who is in a hurry to get away, there is a great likelihood of an undiscussed item being accepted unheard.

But let us not assume that all summarizers are devious and ready to use the pressure of the situation for their own ends. After all, such an incident could occur by accident; the undiscussed item appearing without the summarizer realizing that it has not been cleared. The devious approach has a parallel in negotiations when the final written agreement emerges and does not reflect completely the agreements reached verbally at the negotiation.

PROPOSING

During the course of many types of interview, such as appraisals, project arrangements, development planning etc., in fact every interview in which decisions have to be made, someone has to put forward the ideas. In an ideal situation, the interviewee – normally the subordinate – is to be encouraged to be the proposer. It has been found from both research and practice that if the proposals come from the one who has to put them into practice there is much more commitment to implementation than if they come from the interviewer, usually the boss. There are dangers in forcing an action on somebody else:

- They may have had the same idea, but, given the opportunity, wanted to propose it themselves
- The idea may not fit in with what they are capable of doing or prepared/want to do, but because it is the boss who is saying it, they feel they are unable to disagree
- To have decisions imposed immediately produces an adverse reaction.

One tendency of interviewers is to imagine that they are either in possession of all the possible solutions or that it is they who should always provide the solutions for their subordinates. Neither of these could be true; the first also assumes that the interviewer in addition to all the possible solutions, possesses all the facts about a problem – a very unlikely situation. The second erroneous assumption is linked to the commitment of the subordinate and has been described earlier. There is no requirement on the boss to provide all the solutions; his role is to provide the environment and opportunity for the problem-owner to grow by solving his own problems.

There will be some occasions when, even with the most appropriate techniques, the interviewer (boss) will be unable to draw out ideas from the interviewee (subordinate). A typical session might include:

> Interviewer: 'Well Bill, we've agreed that we need to produce a complete plan for this new product. What ideas have you?'
> Interviewee (confused because of the unexpected turn to him): 'Errr, well hmmmm – I'm sorry, I've no ideas at the moment. This has just come out of the blue and I've no experience of this type of work.'
> Interviewer: 'Oh come on Bill, surely you must have some ideas'.
> Interviewee (feeling even more pressured): 'Well no, sorry. I just can't think.'

It may be essential that the interview finishes with some form of plan, but it is evident that Bill, at the moment, is in no state to initiate any ideas. One option is to adjourn the meeting to allow Bill to collect himself, review what is required and come back with his ideas. This may be successful, but additional time is being used and perhaps the delay may not have been necessary.

One option is for the interviewer to try to get something achieved at the interview and because of the situation he may have to take the initiative temporarily himself. This will allow Bill some time to think and if some clues (not solutions) are given, he will be helped to consider how to progress and thus grow. The interview could progress:

> *Interviewer*: 'OK Bill, it wasn't fair to shoot this at you

out of the blue. One idea I had to start the process
would be . . . . What do you feel about the likely
success of that approach?'
Interviewee: 'Yes, that would be a good starter and I'm
beginning to see what could follow from it'.
Interviewer: 'Right. So if you see some actions which
could ensue, have you any ideas how we could move
from that stage?'
Interviewee: 'One way we might follow that up could
be to . . .'.

The effective interviewer should know when to press for
ideas and keep on pressing, and when to accept that little
will come from the interviewee.

The incidence of proposals is one of the many features of
the decision-making process. Research and observation
have shown that the way the proposal is presented can
affect its success. Peter Honey has analysed many
interactions to determine the likelihood of one specific
behaviour following another. One of the categories of
behaviour which produced significant possibilities was that
of proposing. Honey found that if the proposal was made in
the form of a statement or order, the likelihood of its being
supported was 25 per cent, against the greater likelihood of
being responded to with a disagreement of 39 per cent.

Proposals of this nature can include

Let's do . . .
I propose that we . . .
I think we should . . .
What we must do is . . .

SUGGESTING

However, if the proposal is made in the form of a question
rather than a statement, there is a greater likelihood of it
being supported, 42 per cent, as against 18 per cent
disagreement. Proposals made in this form were described
by Honey as suggestions and can take the form of

What do you think about the idea of . . . ?

The difference in these two approaches is the natural reaction of most people against being told what to do as opposed to their being asked and thus brought into the decision-making process. Of course, there will be occasions when a proposal is the appropriate approach rather than the more informal suggestion, and vice versa. For example, when a new group of people come together for the first time, in the early stages of the group life the members are more likely to be looking for a lead and a direction, rather than be given an open hand. In such a situation, the likelihood of a suggestion producing action is less than if the lead was given in the form of a directive proposal. On the other hand, if we return to the situation described on p. 41 when Bill was unable to supply any ideas at first to the plan, this was where the suggestion would be more likely to be appropriate. If the first lead idea of the interviewer-boss had emerged in the form of a proposal, Bill would probably have sat back and thought 'Great, I'm off the hook. The boss is going to do it.' However, the interviewer could have said simply 'What do you think about the idea of starting the process with . . .?' instead of what he initially said, which was a proposal modified with a question, unfortunately a closed one.

There are so many behaviours which can prove useful in any interview and an equal number which can cause problems.

DISAGREEING

Those so far described have been the more positive behaviours which should help the interaction to progress. On the other hand the interviewer must be aware of the more negative behaviours which exist, how they can upset an interaction, how liable he (the interviewer) is to use them and what the likely reaction might be rather than an appropriate action if they are used by the interviewee.

Disagreeing can be a difficult behaviour because it tends to breed further disagreement and perhaps ultimately conflict between the two people. But disagreements can and must exist otherwise attitudes become unhelpfully non-assertive. We can disagree in two ways. One is almost certain to produce an adverse or unhelpful reaction. The other, although still running that risk, takes some of the sting out of the tail.

If, in response to a suggestion made by someone else, I say 'No, I don't agree', the response by the other might be

- questioning to seek reasons for my disagreement
- withdrawal and no further interaction
- an attack on me for disagreeing in this way.

All these responses are unhelpful in the discussion. The questioning approach appears at first glance to be appropriate behaviour, but if it is taken, my response might still be to disagree and the three options can again be considered by the other. If again the first option is taken, I might be forced to give my reasons and these may be received by a petulant or angry 'Why didn't you say that in the first place?'

The other person might follow the second option, feeling that it isn't even worth finding out why I disagree and consequently the interaction fails.

The third option is more dangerous since it brings both of us into conflict and whatever the eventual result, the consequence is some damage to the interaction.

Although disagreement with what has been said is still present, the disagreement with the person, which is the aspect against which most people react, can be reduced somewhat. If, instead of making blunt disagreement only, I also give my reasons for the disagreement, the other person can concentrate on the reasons rather than react to a personal disagreement. The risk of conflict is consequently reduced by the depersonalization.

On occasions when the interview is between subordinate and boss the non-reaction to the blunt disagreement is most likely. If the boss just disagrees the relationship between the two may be such that the subordinate might think in a non-assertive way 'Who am I to ask the boss "why"?' If the boss gives reasons there is the greater likelihood of the subordinate thinking more positively 'Yes, he's right about that' or even saying 'No boss, I'd thought about those objections and they can be overcome'. Whichever way, the interaction has a much greater chance of continuing to a successful conclusion.

Perhaps one of the main problems of disagreement is the overt use of the verbal statement of disagreement, words which can so easily produce an emotional reaction – 'Who does he think he is to disagree with me?'. There is a substantial case for the view that it may be more appropriate and successful to disagree without using the emotive words. Instead of starting with 'No, I don't agree because . . .', there could be a more favourable reaction to 'When I tried this some time ago, I found it didn't work. What I did was . . .' In this latter example, the potentially emotive words of disagreement need not even be said, the reasons make the disagreement apparent. The disagreement is still there but, at the least, the risk of a negative reaction to the emotive words has been reduced.

In summary, disagree by all means if in fact you do so, but (a) always give your reasons immediately, and (b) if possible, do not use the words 'I disagree' or 'I do not (cannot) agree'.

ATTACKING

Even more damaging to an interaction is attacking behaviour. This is identified by statements which use highly emotive words or phrases, or the tone of voice carries an overtone to normally acceptable words – or a combination of both. If I say 'I might have expected Bill to come out with that sort of stupid remark', Bill is left in no doubt that I am attacking him. His response can be to ignore the attack or to opt out because of it, but he could also attack in return to defend himself. If this level of attack/defend spiral continues it can only terminate in the interview when

- both parties disengage from the interaction which has now failed
- one person backs down, usually by apologizing
- both parties back down with mutual apologies
- the fight stops by mutual agreement, spoken or unspoken, but leaving both parties still aggrieved.

Whatever the method of stopping the spiral of attack/defend, the interaction has been wasted and there is always the risk of more permanent damage happening with the relationship. When this type of situation is imminent and you are the potential attacker the simple way to avoid it is not to initiate the attack (unless it is your deliberate intention to do so for some justifiable reason). If you are the one attacked, remember that it takes two to fight and, unless the provocation is too great for you to ignore, refuse to be drawn into the conflict. This may seem a cowardly approach, but you may lose even more by joining the battle unnecessarily.

Backing down to stop the development of an attack/defend spiral is often described as open behaviour. Apologizing has been cited as one aspect of this. Other examples of it are admitting or accepting responsibility openly for a mistake or omission. In most cases the person exhibiting the open behaviour loses very little by so doing, and in fact is less likely to lose credibility than if the error was not admitted but was eventually discovered by someone else.

Open behaviour can sometimes be used deliberately to defuse a situation with one person admitting responsibility *even when it is the fault of the other*. The defusing in cases such as this is often swift and immediate as the other person, on whom the blame really lies, may feel guilty about the incident and be anxious to make amends. This approach demands care – too frequent use is dangerous particularly when one's boss is involved, because one can earn the (unfounded) reputation of making a lot of mistakes.

INTERRUPTING

A particularly abusive form of inappropriate behaviour is interrupting. This mainly takes the form, in a two person interview, of one person saying something before the other has finished speaking. The interrupter is saying non-verbally to the speaker 'Shut up. I have something to say which is more important than your contribution.' It may be more important, but to take action in this way is highly self-centred and can produce adverse reactions in the other person. But the more significant effect of an interruption is that the interrupter cannot possibly be listening to what the other has been saying. He has probably been so emotionally concerned in thinking about his own views and his intention of expressing them that he was not listening.

Of course, it is almost impossible to avoid all interrupting and perhaps complete avoidance would be inappropriate. The absence of interruption can suggest lack of interest, but an excess brings us to the inescapable conclusion that there must have been diminished listening.

Listening is so important in interviews and certain behaviours indicate that it is occurring, rather than interrupting which is an indicator of possible non-listening.

BUILDING

One important listening-related behaviour is building. A proposal is made which adds value, weight or substance to a proposal made by someone else. For example: 'I suggest that we put the plan into action next week'. A related, additional proposal, or build, might be 'And we could also alert the reserve team to stand by in case the implementation group is not completely ready.' More than one build on an original proposal is quite possible, such as 'Right, and if we start the plan off on Wednesday that will give us time to do both'. And so on.

A little consideration will show that a number of factors are necessary in order to allow people to build:

- the idea is supported
- the builder is interested enough to help the proposer, but above all
- listening has taken place so that the other two factors can occur.

Behavioural analysis shows a minimal incidence of building in most people activities. This is not surprising since so little listening takes place between people. Partial listening usually occurs, but interactors are often only waiting for the other to stop talking (sometimes they do not even wait) so that they can introduce their ideas. Neil Rackham suggested an approach, particularly in group meetings, which is intended to encourage building rather than permit indiscriminate proposing by all members with little reference to each other.

Once a proposal has been made, rather than allow counter-proposals and counter-counter-proposals, members are asked to concentrate their attention and interest on the proposal made. They are asked to consider it and to think of possible ways in which it might be added to and improved rather than look for reasons why it would not work. In this way there is every opportunity for a considerable amount of building to take place. By the time all the building has occurred, many of the other possible proposals will have fallen by the wayside and the original proposal developed into a comprehensive, strong agreement on which little extra work will be necessary following the meeting. In the case of the more usual approach to proposals, because there is a lack of this concentration of interest and help, many agreed proposals need considerable post-meeting action to make them viable. A further bonus with the building style of meeting is that the final agreement is one in which most of the members have had a hand and there is therefore likely to be a considerable amount of commitment to the agreement.

Building, of course, is taking the other important listening-related behaviour of supporting one step further. In order to support the views, concepts or ideas of another person, the essential prerequisite is that these views etc.

have been listened to. Consequently, the overt, stated verbal support will confirm to the speaker that listening has taken place.

BLOCKING

One final significant behaviour which an interviewer will take strongly into account with benefit, is the flippant, facetious remark commonly described by analysts as blocking. There can be little doubt that humour has a significant place in many interactions and it can be particularly useful to relieve tension in some situations. But if this behaviour becomes too frequent and obtrusive, it can have a negative effect and cause the other party to doubt the credibility of the humourist – 'Can this guy really be serious?' In the same way that the attacking, disagreeing and interrupting behaviours have their places in a controlled way, so with blocking. But it must be controlled within an acceptable and appropriate degree. How does one know the acceptable level of the other person? This is one of the serious problems of interactions with someone else, because usually the signals showing the limit has been reached do not appear strongly until the limit has been passed.

If we consider the questioning behaviours described in Chapter 3 and the other behaviours of this chapter, it is obvious that the interviewer has to take more into account than the structure of the interview. He must be aware of the behaviours emerging, what they are and how they can be used, even manipulated. In order to do this he must listen to what is said and be aware of all the contributions being made, both verbal and non-verbal. In any interview something is happening all the time, most of it very important, and the interviewer cannot afford to miss even the smallest detail.

5 Listening

Chapter 4 has already discussed the importance of listening during an interview. This cannot be overstressed – without listening the interview may as well not take place. In spite of protestations to the contrary, all the signs indicate that insufficient listening takes place between the participants in an interaction. How often have we heard said, or have said ourselves: 'Yes, go ahead, I'm listening to you', when in fact only the voice is being heard, not the words?

Effective listening is a discipline in which most of us have to take positive action. It involves concentration on what is being said by the other person, almost to the exclusion of anything else. Unfortunately, in practice we listen for a while, make an assumption about what is being said, and start to make up our mind how we are going to respond and what we are going to say in this response. We cannot be said to be listening fully and because of this we make assumptions about what is being said or about to be said: these assumptions are not always correct and it is here that interactive problems arise.

Numerous clues exist around us to demonstrate that listening is not happening and we should always be aware of them. Chapter 4 suggests that when building and supporting are absent or limited, when disagreement, interrupting and even attacking occur, and there is a very strong imbalance between seeking and giving information, then listening is suspect. We should be able to identify these behaviours or the absence of them in the contributions of others. We have also to ask ourselves whether we are internally blind and are not recognizing them in our own behaviours.

BARRIERS

Even with initial motivation and the discipline to listen, there are a number of factors working against our effective listening. The most common is the internal dialogue we are having when others are talking to us. While they talk, we are deciding our stance to what they are saying, what we are going to say and rehearsing how we are going to say it. This restriction to our listening can occur because

- we are not really interested in their views
- we are completely opposed to what we think they are saying
- we have decided what they are saying and are only interested in making our own contribution.

Although the mind is capable of thinking much faster than the rate at which most people speak, it does not mean that it is capable of doing both things at the same time – effectively thinking *and* listening.

Physical environment

The physical environment of the interview can contribute to the listening, particularly concerning comfort. An uncomfortable chair, sunlight directly in the eyes, poor air conditioning – all these factors contribute to a reduction in concentration. Conversely, if there is too much comfort, over-relaxation may encourage drowsiness and once again reduced listening. So the preparations discussed in Chapter 2 are not solely concerned with the comfort of the interviewee, but also so that the interviewer is in a suitable environment for listening.

Human states

Two human states, the mind and the body, will affect the
ability to listen. If the interviewer's mind is not completely
attuned to the interview, listening may become a problem.
For example, stressful problems such as finance, housing,
relations, marriage, divorce, family illness etc. might come
to mind even while the interviewee is talking. In fact, it may
be the interviewee's word or phrase which triggers the
interviewer's internal problem dialogue.

Similarly, the state of the interviewer's body can affect
his powers of concentration. Something as simple as an
unreachable itch, stomach ache, headache or fatigue can
all have an inhibiting and debilitating effect and reduce
listening.

The value judgements of an interviewer can certainly
impede listening, again if a word or phrase of the
interviewee triggers some otherwise suspended thought.
Suppose the interviewer had recently been involved in an
argument with a neighbour. A trigger in this case might be
the interviewee mentioning a conflict with his own
neighbour. In consequence the interviewer's own problem
may temporarily take precedence with a resultant
reduction in listening.

Memory can also create problems. Different people
have different levels of ability in absorbing and retaining
information. If the interviewer is relying solely on his
memory during the interview, apart from the actual
forgetting of detail which can create other problems in the
interview, the retrieval of data can have an effect on
listening. While the data banks are being searched to
retrieve information given perhaps earlier in the interview,
concentration on the 'here and now' lapses, listening is
reduced and further information is missed.

Not all speakers, and particularly some interviewees
who may be in a strong emotional state, are articulate and
at times the interviewer may interrupt his own listening by
thinking 'What does he mean by that statement?'. So we
have yet another barrier, the act of interpretation
disturbing the listening pattern.

The list of potential barriers lengthens! Another barrier problem which pertains to the interviewer, concerns his attitude towards the interviewee. This barrier may be more common when the interviewee is a stranger to the interviewer. Once the interviewee has started talking the interviewer might react in a negative way to what is being said because of an immediate assumption that the material is uninteresting, or it has all been heard before, or the interviewer feels he knows what the interviewee is going to say.

Linked to the content delivery of the interviewee is the manner in which the delivery is made. If the physical conditions of post-lunch apathy combine with a long-winded, boring interviewee, the interviewer can have an internal fight to retain an active listening interest. Even mannerisms of the interviewee can be a distraction. I once became so interested in what the interviewee was doing, unconsciously, with a loose thread on his suit that I failed to listen to what he was saying – fortunately to one of the other members of the interview panel!

Selective listening

Sometimes we can be accused of selective listening, of seeking views which we want to hear and behaviours we want to see, or ignoring those we do not want to see or hear. This is common in selection or promotion interviews. We are all prone to having first impressions of people, those which we gain within a short time of meeting someone for the first time. There is a strong lobby of opinion which suggests that, however long the interaction continues, people's decisions or views are made in the first five minutes, or perhaps an even shorter period. The remainder of the time which should be taken up in really getting to know the person is, albeit subconsciously, used in securing evidence to support the first impression. This means that we hear only those statements or views that we wish to hear and may even twist other statements to make them fit our stereotype.

One psychological factor is known as the 'halo' effect. We associate people with our own views of them because for example 'they look like us so therefore they must be OK'. Here again we can look for and listen for only those things we want to see and hear, and will reject or twist the remainder. Consequently real listening will have taken a back seat.

Conversely, if our first impression is negative, for whatever reasons, the danger is that we shall look selectively for damning features only, again in order to support our stereotype.

Research aside, these effects may be more widespread than we have considered. Many people will say that this does not happen with them and that they always wait until they get to know a person before making a decision and listening to their views. This may in fact be so, given the time to vary what might have been the first impression. But unfortunately we do not always have this time. What happens when time is limited? One would hope that either the first impression does not form a lasting influence, or that no first impression is formed. I believe that these two moves are rare and that we are influenced more than we are aware.

Think about interactions you have had with relatively new acquaintances. Have you ever thought after they have said something with which you did not particularly agree 'Well, they didn't really mean it to come out like that' or, conversely, 'They mean more than they are really saying'. These reactions are often the behavioural compensation to satisfy the stereotype or impression and they make a nonsense of any opportunity for listening.

Concentration

The final barrier to listening is concerned with the speed of operation of the mind. The mind can operate faster than a person can talk. It works at the equivalent of more than 500 words per minute. Many people who are skilled in speedreading do so at this rate or more, so their minds must be capable of unrestricted thoughts at an even higher rate. Most speakers talk at between 130 and 150 words per minute which suggests that there is an unused capacity for the mind of, say, 350 words per minute.

This mental gap can explain why our listening attention can wander, because the greater capacity for concentration is unused.

OVERCOMING BARRIERS

So much for the barriers, but how can we overcome them? Consider the barrier just discussed – under-use of the mind. The simple answer is to give the mind something to do to make it concentrate on what is happening.

Notetaking

The listener must discipline himself to concentrate on listening and analysing what is heard. But sometimes more than this is necessary. The additional mind exercise can often be fulfilled by notetaking. In addition to ensuring concentration, the committing to paper may clarify any complexity in what you have heard and thus aid comprehension. The latter benefit will be particularly evident if a 'key word' method of notetaking is used. Instead of writing notes in the traditional manner by making sentences, the key factors of what is being said are identified and key words or short phrases related to these factors make up the notes. For example:

        Alcoholic – he accepts
        Drinking – two years excessive
                beer → spirits → everything/anything
        AA club – 2 weeks – closed
        Wants to dry out
        What to do? 1 . . . . Interested
                     2 . . . . No
                     3 . . . . Possible, etc

The approach to notetaking need not necessarily follow this type of pattern, but it has a number of advantages:

- requires identification of the key aspects
- takes little time to write
- further information can be added to early notes as the interview progresses
- the little amount of writing is less likely to disturb the speaker.

The technique does require some practice. Initially many people, although identifying the key aspects, find it difficult to construct the key words and phrases quickly. Consequently they write down far too many words and the listening actually suffers.

In order to avoid slowness in constructing key words and phrases, a practice which becomes easier with experience, some people find it useful to construct a number of personal or standardized abbreviations in preference to the recognized shorthand or speedscripts.

Some simple abbreviations include:

+ or & – and	c – see or sea
ε – the speed version of e or E	q – queue
	/ – the
y – why	1 – one
u – you	2 – to or too
ur – your	4 – for
b – be	⌐g – 'ing' ending
r – are	⌐n – 'ion' ending

Remember also the standard abbreviations or literary conventions in common use:

eg – for example
ie – that is
cf – Compare(d) with
∴ – therefore
∵ – because
= – is the same as, equals
≠ – is not the same as, does not equal
≏ – approximately equals

→ - lead to, progresses to
\> - is greater than
\< - is less than

It may be considered fashionable to denigrate abbreviations and jargon, but these notes are generally for
your use and benefit. If, however they are to be used by
others then the criticism may apply, and they will have to
be rewritten in a form which will be acceptable to and
readable by the recipient.

In certain cases, for example in disciplinary interviews, it
will be desirable or perhaps even a requirement to make
the abbreviated notes into full textual notes. The benefit of
this approach when desirability is the criterion will be that
when the notes are read at some future date, perhaps after
a long interval, the abbreviations and key words may not
mean as much as they did at the time of the incident. If
formal disciplinary procedures are being followed, it may
be necessary eventually for others to read the notes,
including the person about whom the notes were made.

The concept of key words and phrases is used not only in
the traditional format of vertically laid out notes, but also in
the patterned notetaking technique pioneered by Tony
Buzan in his television series which was accompanied by a
useful BBC publication, *Use Your Head*. The patterned
note is very similar to the vertically constructed format in
the use of key words and phrases except that these notes
emerge from a central point and spread around this centre.
Figure 5.1 is an example of a pattern of this nature, using
the vertically presented key words suggested earlier.

The principal practical advantages of the patterned
approach are that the pattern can usually be contained on
one side of an A4 sheet of paper; linking themes can be
shown (the ←→ in the pattern example); and drawings and
colours can be included more easily. These are in addition,
of course, to the basic difference from vertical notes in that
our minds work in patterns rather than in a vertical,
rational, logical manner.

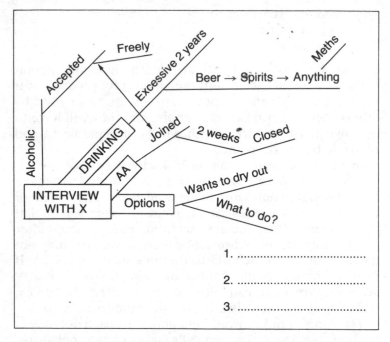

Figure 5.1　A patterned note

Because we have started to develop a constructive approach to listening, let us continue in this vein. But first Figure 5.2 summarizes what we have considered so far:

Notetaking will obviously not be the only method of trying to overcome the barriers to listening. Many of the other means will simply be the reversal as far as possible of the barrier factors which can be summarized as follows:

Prepare for the interview and prepare to listen.
Be interested in what is being said.
Ignore one's own opposition to views being expressed.
Do not try to forecast what the other is going to say.
Ensure that all the physical factors have been considered – light, heat, ventilation etc.
Be aware of one's own value judgements and take these into account.
Develop a receptive state of mind.

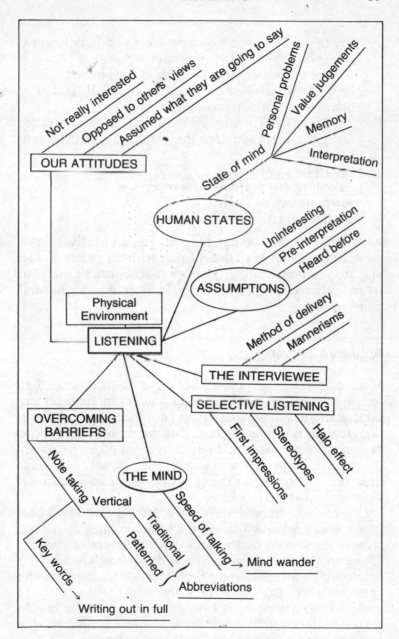

Figure 5.2   A summary

Try to put aside one's own problems – otherwise have somebody else take the interview.
Do not make assumptions early in the interview.
Listen to what is being said and do not be distracted by delivery or mannerisms.
Try not to form immediate impressions – but if you do, recognize them for what they are and take them into account.
Listen for key issues.
Take notes to avoid mind wander.
Maintain eye contact.
Do not interrupt.

Although you may be listening fully and effectively, this may not be apparent to the speaker with the result that he may stop communicating. Two approaches can be useful to let the other know you are actively listening – verbal and non-verbal.

Apparent listening

Most of the verbal approaches have been discussed in previous chapters – asking questions, clarifying, testing understanding, summarizing; and not blocking, attacking, disagreeing, nor interrupting. But the non-verbal actions may be more important than the verbal ones. Certainly they need to be present and also must be apparent. There is little use in listening to the other person if he cannot tell whether you are in fact listening.

One of the most common ways of letting a speaker know that you are actually listening is to use continuity noises, sometimes known as the non-verbal aspects of speech. These are the 'yeahs', 'mmmms' and 'uh huhs' which can be employed by the listener and are intended to convey to the speaker that (a) you are listening, (b) you are understanding what he is saying and (c) you want him to carry on talking. If they are absent, the speaker is receiving no signals nor clues to your internal reactions.

On one occasion I had to attend a promotion interview where the chairman of the panel was supported by two other interviewers. I was passed to one of the sidesmen by the chairman and this interviewer asked me what my views were about a certain current aspect – a good open question. I started my reply, but as I talked I looked at the questioner who looked back at me completely poker-faced. Not a flicker of reaction crossed his face and soon I began to wonder whether (a) I had heard the question correctly, (b) I was giving an answer which was acceptable and (c) I was talking too much! The final question became the most important one to me, so I stopped talking and was immediately attacked with 'Well, is that all you have to say about it?'. Fortunately when I was passed to the other sidesman, there were a reasonable number of noises coming from him which I interpreted as signals to continue talking. I felt much more settled at that stage than during the earlier period of the interview and I knew to some extent the effect I was having, rather than wishing the ground would open up and swallow me!

On the other hand these continuity noises can be overdone to the extent that there are so many of them that the listener cannot possibly hear what the speaker is saying; they can be a habit.

I recall two particular incidents when this excess of non-verbal signals produced a negative effect. During a training course a group was discussing a subject under the elected chairmanship of one of their fellows. During the discussion, of which I was an observer, the chairman kept up a constant production of noises and from my observations of non-verbal glances and other signals by the remainder of the group, it was obvious they too had remarked on these. At the end of the activity, during the subsequent discussion about how it had been performed, it emerged that all the group had been disturbed by these noises, had felt that he had held back the discussion in this way, and at least two of the group had almost attacked him because of this. The unfortunate chairman's response was that he had not realized what he had been doing and it was obviously an unconscious habit (which could have had unfortunate consequences).

On another occasion an interviewer had the unconscious habit of saying 'good' as a continuity noise rather than as an expression of his feelings. This was fine until one day the interviewee said 'and then my father died' upon which he heard the response 'Good'!

The principal non-verbal signals during an interaction are given by the face. They include the movement of the mouth into a smile or otherwise, the movement of the eyebrows, nods or shakes of the head. These signals all suggest reactions by the listener or one person to the other, and their absence can raise questions, doubts and suspicion.

The eyes are perhaps more expressive than anything else and in particular the direction in which they are looking. It does not need psychological research to tell us that, in the case of most people, if we are listening to somebody we look at them for most of the time that they are talking. We do not look at them *all* the time because such a permanent gaze, except in the case of lovers soon becomes an embarrassment. But normal observation, supported by psychological research, shows that we do in fact look directly at each other for some 60 per cent of the time if we are interested. If we are not interested this feeling is usually transmitted by the wandering gaze, our eyes returning to the speaker for a short period only then wandering away again.

One of the problems with non-verbal signals is that being seen they need to be interpreted. A person receiving a message may look at the speaker, apparently as if listening is taking place. In fact, the eye-contact may be only a pose. Behind the pose, albeit a very effective one, the receiver is not really listening. However, unless there are other signals, the only interpretation possible is one of listening.

The eyes and the area around them emit other signals which can be added together to confirm the listening signal. When we are interested in someone or in what they are saying, in addition to looking at them most of the time, the pupils of the eyes tend to dilate, whereas if the 'listener' is far away the well-known glazed look appears in the eyes.

However, either of these effects can be simulated by someone who is intent on giving a particular impression.

Linked with the eyes is the mouth, another potentially expressive part of the face. When someone is talking to us, unless the subject is very serious or objectionable, we tend to smile at them from time to time, thus implying 'Go on. I'm with you. I'm listening'. But some smiles, usually those when a deliberate pose is being presented, begin and end with the mouth, whereas real smiles can often be identified by an associated 'smile in the eyes'.

The eyes and mouth, because they are so expressive, need to be seen in order that the signals might be recognized. Consider the problems in having a conversation with a person wearing dark glasses so that we cannot see their eyes. Many of us feel uncomfortable talking to a blind person because of this lack of eye contact. Similarly with the mouth: the signalling movements can only mean something if they can be seen. Problems arise when the mouth is hidden, usually by the hand.

The whole body can transmit similar signals – alert or bored. The alert signals are usually given by the listener sitting reasonably upright and straight, and often leaning forward slightly. On the other hand, a slumped pose can suggest boredom or lack of interest. However, like most non-verbal signals one has to be careful in the interpretation, because the reverse may sometimes be the case, the reversed poses signifying an opposite attitude to the normal interpretation.

In Chapter 2 the orientation factor was shown to have an effect on attitudes, often from the selection of seating positions. Similar signals can be given by the nearness or otherwise that one stands or sits to the other person. Everybody has what is known as proxemic zones, the area surrounding a person which is treated as his own private area. This area is guarded jealously and others are only allowed within if the owner wants this intrusion. If the personal zone is invaded, the space owner takes action to repel the invasion usually by moving away slightly. Friendly gestures, including listening can be signified by movement towards the boundary of the personal zone but without the privacy invasion. Conversely, movement away from the person into the outer more formal zone can be a signal of unwillingness to interact.

Finally, the behaviour which above all suggests that listening is not taking place is an interruption before the speaker has finished. As suggested in Chapter 4, the interrupter is telling the other that he has something more important to say and, not only that, but he has stopped listening to the speaker so that he can make his contribution. The remedy for this type of behaviour is in the action of not interrupting and also the more positive exercise of *not wanting* to interrupt. This can be achieved only by really listening to what is being said, being interested in the views of others and concentrating on these stimuli.

It will be apparent that, for an interviewer, listening is as important a behaviour as talking, possibly more important on most occasions – certainly in those situations when it is necessary to extract as much as possible from the interviewee. As an interviewer there is a physical fact we might consider. If Nature had intended us to talk more than we listen, we would have two mouths and one ear rather than the other way round! A facetious comment perhaps, but one which attempts to put the two important factors into a true balance.

6 Levels of interviewing

The important and various methods of questioning during interviews have been considered in Chapter 3. However, other factors are involved in the effectiveness of the questions, not only in the way they are posed, but also in the sensitivity of this questioning. Indeed this aspect of questioning could be considered more important than what might be described as the mechanics of the approach. Misinterpretation of what is intended at this subjective level can cause more failures of interactions than any other activity or intervention. If, for example, the questioning attempts to probe the deepest levels of feeling before the interviewee is ready to talk at these levels, the interviewee may close up completely and not even disclose information at the shallowest levels.

Many models concerned with questioning levels have been produced, all with a similar basic theme and none particularly original, other than putting a recognized and appropriate practice into words. The basis of these models is the recognition of the different viewpoints taken by people in the same situation.

When a number of people go to a party, many of them will have different reasons and motives for attending, that is different viewpoints. Some may be there for the food, some for conversation, some for drink and yet others for the development of relationships. This question of viewpoints was raised in Chapter 3 where a group of people who were all standing on the same mountain summit had different individual views resulting from their permanent or temporary viewpoints on life – colour emphasis; shape emphasis; people orientation; self-interest etc. This variation is quite natural in view of the variations between people, not only in the way they think and react internally, but also as a result of external influences on them.

When we approach people in an open manner, in the same way that the mountain top viewpoints will vary, so can the reactions of individuals.

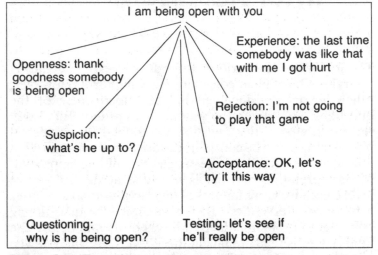

Figure 6.1   Reactions to the open approach

Figure 6.1 shows some of the possible varied reactions in an interactive situation between two people, the mountain top viewpoints being translated into personal reactions to an initiating contribution in which the speaker makes the offer of openness.

The anticipated reaction is that the open offer is accepted in the way in which it was intended and as a quite natural and easy response. The general advice given for the improvement or maintenance of interactive relationships is that openness will breed openness. If you play your cards close to your chest, the other person is most likely to do the same and no progress will be made in the relationship or the exchange of feedback. This approach will work in many cases and situations, but not every situation will result in reactions of this desired manner. However, unless there are clear indications to the contrary, most occasions will benefit from this approach until evidence is available that it is not helping.

On the contrary, the open approach may be met with outright suspicion – 'What's he up to?'. This may be the first occasion on which the individual has been treated in this way, the usual approach being closed and directive. Any change from the norm tends to raise suspicion until people are completely sure that there is no danger for them in the new situation. With some the closed way of life is so inbuilt that it would take a long time and a lot of effort to achieve the desired reaction; perhaps it would never occur.

A rather similar reaction to that of suspicion occurs when experience plays its part. The respondent may have previously responded openly to an apparently open approach, only to be hurt in the experience. The initial approach may have been overtly open, but covertly fooling the respondent into placing himself in a vulnerable position. In a case such as this the initiator will be required to prove that the openness is in fact genuine.

Less extreme than the suspicious reaction is the more normal questioning approach common to most people who want to know why such an open manner is being exhibited. The questions which arise in the individual's thinking are

Why is he behaving like that?
What does he want me to do?
How does he want me to respond?

The opposite viewpoint to the open, accepting one is outright rejection of the approach, usually by those who never behave in this manner themselves and consequently are going to have nothing to do with those who do. Quite often this group is synonymous with those who have had bad experiences, but otherwise it could be an inbuilt state of mind.

When the open approach is not rejected, there is a halfway house between that state and complete acceptance. There are those to whom the approach tends to appeal, but they are a little unsure about reacting

completely openly – 'OK, let's try it this way (but I am ready
to react the other way if things go wrong)'. Taking this
approach a little further is the tester who is interested in
determining how far the open person will go in the
openness.

Many different behaviours will be received in a like
manner as a result of the different viewpoints and reactions
of different people. The principal problem with
interactions is the awareness of which reaction you are
likely to produce, or being aware during the interaction of
the varying reactions through time. The best we can hope
to do, if there is no evidence as to what the reaction will be,
is to try a moderate approach and develop it progressively,
watching very carefully for any signs of rejection or non-
acceptance.

The natural progression of an interview utilizes this
awareness and testing approach, moving through the
various levels as the signals suggest appropriateness. My
own preference from the many models of questioning
levels is based on a four-level approach. However,
although these levels can represent a progressive ladder of
penetration, the obvious progression does not always have
to be followed slavishly.

FOUR-LEVEL QUESTIONING

Level 1, the lowest level of penetration, represents the type
of questioning which is most common in the early stages of
an interaction when the participants are just starting to get
to know each other. At this stage, information only is
sought in a straightforward, non-threatening way and
much of the interaction is relatively superficial. In an
appraisal interview, a typical level 1 question might be
'What is the range of duties you perform?'. Under normal
circumstances this question will produce a general
response describing factually the work performed. This
type of discussion which can continue for some time, is
non-threatening and does not challenge the interviewee
either from a fact or a value point of view. Consequently

the interviewee is led over familiar ground and is thus encouraged to talk freely. Few people can resist the invitation to talk about their work – the biggest problem often is to stop them! There is a danger, however, that if this level is maintained for too long a period, the interviewee becomes too comfortable and may resist eventual efforts to raise the level of the questioning.

In the early stages of an interview, most people give information at the fairly superficial level and if real information is required other approaches need to be introduced. If more sensitive information is required the interviewer often needs to probe the initial answers. Such probing, level 2 questions, following the level 1 question suggested above, might start with 'I see. And which of these duties you have told me about take more of your time than others?'. This question is deeper than level 1 since it seeks disclosure of information which may not be completely factually based and which may have some degree of sensitivity involved. In fact, on some occasions the questioner may not even have to attempt this relatively low level of questioning as the interviewee may not wish to be probed.

The gap between levels 2 and 3 is quite large as the level 3 questions extend the probing into more potentially sensitive areas and take the interaction beyond the purely factual into the early areas of opinions, thoughts and views. But at this stage any probing into these areas does not attempt to penetrate deep feelings, the real areas of extreme sensitivity. Even at the relatively shallow level of feelings sensitivity the approaches can easily be rejected. Following our level 1 and 2 questions, the one at level 3 would be something like 'Which of these duties do you enjoy doing the most?'.

Many interactions do not need to progress any deeper than level 3. If the interviewer wants to go deeper he must be satisfied that the interviewee also wishes to do so. Usually some verbal clues are given by the interviewee and the interviewer must be alert for those. Questions at level 4 may be 'Why do you enjoy doing x?' and 'How do you feel about the other duties you have to do?'. These invite the interviewee to express his value judgements and the significant words at this level are 'Why' and 'Feel'.

An interaction between two people can be logged as to the levels involved in the same way that one can use some form of interaction analysis. An example of part of an interaction is shown in Figure 6.2 and this log represents about ten minutes of the interaction. The interaction was intended to bring out the views of the interviewee on a subject in which she had a particular interest. The top line shows the numbered sequence of the transactions, the lower line the level of the contribution. On this lower line, the responses of the interviewee are shown in bold type.

1	2	3	4	5	6	7	8	9	10	11	12	13	14	15	16
1	**1**	**1**	**1**	**1**	**2**	**2**	**2**	**2**	**2**	3	**2**	1	**2**	**2**	**2(3)**

17	18	19	20	21	22	23	24	25	26	27	28	29	30
3	**3**	**3**	**3**	1	**1**	2	**2**	3	3	2	**2**	2	**2**

31	32	33	34	35	36	
3	**3**	4	**1**	1	**2**	....

Figure 6.2   Interaction analysis

An analysis of this interaction log shows a natural start to the interview with interactions 1 to 5 all at the superficial level 1 of seeking and obtaining information. The interviewer was quite content to leave the discussion for the time being at this level. But the attitude of the interviewer and the non-threatening early approach must have given the interviewee encouragement for response 6 was a voluntary raising of the level to level 2. Fortunately the interviewer was listening intently and was in tune with the responses he was receiving. Consequently the raising of the level message was picked up and the interviewer responded with a level 2 contribution. And so the interaction continued at this rather higher level until at transaction 11 the interviewer tried to raise the level to level 3 with a question of that nature. Apparently, from the level 2 response at 12, the interviewee was not ready for this, but still felt sufficiently comfortable to respond at level 2 rather than force the issue back to level 1. However, the interviewer panicked at the response which was different from that expected and himself took flight at 13 to the safe level 1 contribution. The interviewee remained comfortable in the level 2 atmosphere and retained this level in the response at 14. In the latter part of the interviewee's response at 16 a clue was given that she would be willing to progress to a deeper level.

The interviewer at transaction 17 recognized this clue and took up the offer with a level 3 contribution; at which level the discussion continued to transaction 20 when, because some new information had emerged, the interviewer had to return to level 1 questioning. A fluctuating pattern of levels 1, 2 and 3 continued the interview until at transaction 33 the interviewer attempted a level 4 question. Once again, however, the interviewee was not ready for this fairly significant change of level and in fact took flight back to level 1. And so the interview continued. For those readers who like happy endings, the final transactions of the interview were 4,4,4,4!

The principal lessons emerging from this case study involving the levels of interaction include

- When in doubt, start at level 1 and follow a natural progression
- Listen to the responses
- Be alert for clues and cues which suggest that the other is willing to move to a deeper level
- Be alert for clues and cues which suggest that you have to back off and revert to a lower level
- Do not move to a higher level, particularly level 4, unless it is evident that both parties are ready.

BEHAVIOUR v INTERNAL MOTIVATION

A question which frequently occurs in the minds of interaction participants, particularly the interviewer, is why the other person is reacting or behaving in a certain mode or manner. At the start of the interaction, for example, all the indications may be that a deep and revealing relationship could develop. But as it progresses it becomes evident that this is not to be. Or during an event which has been progressing well, the atmosphere and reaction suddenly changes and deteriorates. Why?

There is one school of thought which suggests we should not ask the deep and searching question 'why' since we may not penetrate to the root of the problem, or even worse, we may obtain answers which may not reflect the real reasons. When we are told something, particularly about the feelings of the person concerned, in the absence of any other evidence we *must* accept what we are told, even though the person giving us that information is deliberately not telling the truth. Instead of asking 'why' with all the risks involved, we should be asking 'what' – 'What happened immediately before this change?', 'What did I say/do to cause this different behaviour?', 'What is happening now?' and 'What should I do now?'.

In other words, because we may not get to the internal reasoning, we should go for the behaviour, the overt evidence of success or failure. However, asking the historical behavioural questions 'What did I say/do?' will lead you back to a point in the interaction when it may have been *your* behaviour, either in an initiatory or reactive way which caused the other person to behave in the observed manner. The remedy for the interaction failure, unless it has gone too far to be remedied, is then to exhibit behaviour which will bring the interaction back to the required level.

This approach in no way reflects adversely on any of the other techniques discussed since the basis of the interaction is still full listening and awareness of the whole situation. It does save the problems of trying to obtain or interpret the reasons which a person might have for doing something, concentrating rather on what is done. After all, we do not react to a person's inner thoughts, only to the overt exhibition of those thoughts, the behaviour. We can consider our part in the interaction with others. How many times have we been asked 'Are you feeling OK?', to which we answer 'Yes of course', even when we might be feeling far from it.

We can of course obtain feedback about motivation and internal reasoning when we are considering our own actions, but even this gives us indications of the difficulties of discovering them in others – do we always know ourselves *why* we are saying or doing something?

The approach described in this chapter demonstrates that there is more to interviewing than the straightforward, formal and traditional structures. It is necessary on most occasions to try to delve deeper than the superficial level and attempt to assess the internal attitudes, feelings and motivations of both yourself, the interviewer and the person being interviewed. A difficult area but one which can help to make the interaction more meaningful and help to make it more successful.

7 Problem solving

One of the many responsibilities of the manager is to ensure that the problems of the people who report to him, e.g. junior managers, are solved, or that he himself solves them. Whether it is the manager or someone else who has to solve the problem will usually depend on its seriousness or extent.

Furthermore, the problem can be identified according to its nature; whether it is a technical situation which requires a solution or whether the source of the problem is related to people and their behaviour.

Problems of the first type, the technical or procedural differences, require in the main a logical, rational, technical approach – Why does the machine stop so frequently? How does the produce mover behave in this irregular manner? Why is the computer rejecting the new program? And so on. Solutions normally will follow a logical, fault-finding pattern similar to the actions of a motor mechanic when a car breaks down, rather than dart from one part of the mechanism to another without any reason. Procedures of this nature are usually based on experience which has shown that a logical approach will save diagnostic time. Clues will lead the repairer to perhaps one area rather than another: if the car engine cuts out completely without warning, the avenue of fault-finding may be an electrical one rather than a mechanical or fuel one. The logical path will start at the electrical source, the battery, and the fault-finder will tend thence to follow the system through such parts as the coil, distribution, plugs and leads.

However, many problems are people-based and it is to this aspect that the interactive manager addresses himself. The techniques and methods described in this book are all directed to the solving of problems of this nature. If a person has misbehaved, the approach is through discipline; if the problem originates with the worker as a complaint, a grievance interview will result, and so on. But the interaction only provides the vehicle for the problem-solving approach and the variety of interactive events only serves to pinpoint the absence of a logical, fault-finding method similar to that described above. There are too many variables for such a method to exist – people!

Most of the people problems encountered have their roots firmly embedded in behaviour – what a person does, how they do it, with whom they do it, etc. In most cases, the problem involves more than one person, for after all individual behaviour is almost invariably the result of the behaviour of another person or persons. The basic principle of interactions between people is that whatever someone does or does not do to someone else, a behavioural response is produced in the other, whether this is a positive or a negative behaviour or even no apparent behaviour at all. It has been said that behaviour breeds behaviour or, expressed in a different form, if you do something to me, I shall react in some way. If someone walks up to me and hits me on the nose, I shall either

- Hit back
- Stand there and cry (and bleed)
- Run away
- Ask the reason for the attack
- Do nothing actively by just standing there (but all sorts of thoughts will be running through my mind)

and so on.

If I am treated in a pleasant friendly way, I am likely to react in the same manner. If I am insulted for no apparent reason, I can react angrily or perhaps in a puzzled way. So for any action there will usually be some form of reaction, overt or covert. The non-reaction can be observed as a reaction in itself. For example, if a proposition is made to another person at a party and the approach is met by silence, it will appear that the approach has been rejected.

Consequently, behaviour must be recognized as having considerable value and importance since it is the keystone of all interactions between people. Obviously the overt behavioural actions and reactions are not everything which may be occurring. Earlier in this book we considered the motivation encouraged or controlled by the individual's ego states or modes. Even if this model cannot be fully accepted, we do not need to be psychologists or psychiatrists to realize that external behaviour is not the only driving force of an individual. The behaviour can be considered to be the tip of an iceberg, the part which is visible, the part which people can hear and see. But there is much more under the surface, much more that we are not allowed to see or allow others to see. With people, below the surface are feelings, attitudes, thoughts, motives, all of which are the prime factors behind the behaviour.

However, it is only the behaviour which is seen by us and to which we react. If we see an angry man, we react in some way to this *expressed* anger. What we do not know is whether this anger is real or artificially induced, what thoughts or feelings are surging within the person, even perhaps why the anger has arisen. Of course, we can ask the person for reasons, feelings, thoughts etc. and we may receive a reply which purports to give us this internal information. Unfortunately we cannot be 100 per cent certain that what we are being told is the truth. There may be other indicators or other behaviours which will help us to confirm or deny these statements, but even with these apparent supporters we still cannot say what is really going on behind the visible facade.

These doubts suggest that we must rely principally on overt behaviour to give us our views on the actions and reactions of others, because anything else must be considered too subjective to allow us to make a complete assessment. If an aeroplane crashes onto our house, we know *what* has happened, but we do not know (or perhaps even care) *why* it has happened. The approach to solving problems related to people must therefore be behaviourally anchored – any other information must be treated as a bonus.

PROBLEM-SOLVING MODELS

There are various models and approaches to solving problems, both people and non-people problems. Some of these are highly sophisticated and no doubt successful if they are followed. But many of them are so complex that they only have a place in an academic text-book on problem solving. Their very complexity works against their being used except as academic exercises. I have been involved with training courses which include models of this nature and I have been impressed by them, but I have never used them in practice when I have returned to work. On occasions I have been so impressed by a particular model that I have introduced it to managers on a training course. The model was equally successful on the course and the managers were obviously impressed. However, at a later stage after the course, when I asked the managers whether any of them had used the model or even parts of it, the answer was a universal 'no' for the reasons I have stated above. With most people the effective principle must be 'Keep it simple', otherwise, however excellent, the model is commended but ignored. After all, whether we like to admit it or not, the majority of decisions are made in practice and followed by the rationalization of reasons why that was the correct decision!

Consequently my preference has always been for a model with four steps only!

1 What is the behaviour being exhibited in the present (problem) situation?
2 What is happening when this problem behaviour is being exhibited?
3 What is the desired situation or behaviour?
4 What behavioural change can be brought about to produce the desired effects?

This model is not as simple as it has just been expressed. When one looks at the detail, it is more complex, but the complexities will depend on the problem solver rather than the model.

STAGE 1   IDENTIFICATION OF THE PROBLEM

The method of identifying the problem will vary with the nature of the problem, but it will always have its base in a description of the problem – an incident or behaviour which differs from the practice or behaviour which has been defined (by somebody) and the definition accepted as efficient, effective, correct or acceptable. If someone or something is not operating to this defined criterion, we have a 'problem'. The technical problems are in many ways the simplest to identify:

- A machine which has been operating efficiently starts to behave erratically
- A computer rejects a new program
- The monthly accounts do not balance.

Rather more difficult to assess are the situations which are not quite so clear cut:

- If the monthly statistics do not reflect the anticipated projection there is an immediate and perhaps more basic problem
  (a) the statistical trend may be correct
  (b) the statistics may be incorrect.

The problems relating to people are manifold and can range from

- the production of insufficient/inaccurate work
- bad timekeeping
- being argumentative whenever approached with a request
- always refusing to admit to/ covering up mistakes
- paying too much /little attention to detail
- being aggressive with boss/colleagues/subordinates

- being too demanding of others
- being cold and distant.

It will be readily seen that when we come to the people-related problems it is more difficult to state a simple identification without more definition than for the technical problems. It becomes more difficult to pinpoint even the initial problem and the important action at this stage is to state, re-state and perhaps re-re-state to define the problem as accurately as possible.

Let us take as an example that last-quoted problem: 'He is too cold and distant'. In such a case we need further information to pinpoint the real problem base and hence its effects. With whom is he cold and distant? Is it with everybody? Is it only we who consider him so or is this a universal feeling? What effect is this behaviour having? (Is there really a problem?) And so on. A similar approach can be taken with the other cited 'problems' of aggressiveness, being too demanding etc.

It is possible to list a range of words which are commonly used to identify and describe problems encountered with people, but which in themselves are insufficient with which to commence a problem-solving approach. A typical list would include:

Not motivated	Disruptive
Lazy	Finicky
Aggressive	Disagreeable
Too quiet	Helpless
Poor attitude	Overreactive
Careless	

When considering the subject of problem solving it is easy to be aware of the ineffectiveness of words such as these, but unfortunately their use occurs only too often in real life and others expect us to realize immediately the nature of the problem. This is because in describing people we tend to look for an apparently simple and all-embracing term, particularly when there are a number of people. Many organizations have an annual appraisal system, part of which is the completion of a written report on each person.

If this task is not taken seriously or there are too many
reports to write, the easiest path is to ascribe these general
statements rather than to think more deeply and describe
the person in a more personal and individual detail.
However, on consideration it becomes very clear that two
people, both of whom are described as awkward, are two
completely different individuals with vastly different ways
of demonstrating their 'awkwardness'.

A second common element in the description of people-
related problems is the immediate assumption on the part
of the problem solver about the underlying attitudes of the
problem person. For example, it is easy when observing
someone who does only a little work, not only to say that
they are lazy but also that they are inherently lazy – a
permanent attitudinal feature. In fact there may be many
reasons for this appearance – they may be unwell, under
stress, reacting against some person or incident, etc. This
too ready an assumption of the person's underlying
attitude masks the issue and prevents a real analysis of the
situation.

An individual's behaviour or effect may often be caused
by some personality or attitudinal defect, rather than by
the direct result of some action. In such a case, and the
manager must be absolutely certain that this is so, little can
be done (only a magician is able to change someone's
personality!). However, even in the case of personality
defects there are usually external factors which encourage
the defects to emerge. If someone's permanent personality
defect is irritability, even this is not present for twenty-four
hours a day and surfaces only when the irritation is
triggered. Also, not every event will trigger this aspect of
behaviour, otherwise the person would soon become
exhausted through continuous emotional expression.

The paths to understanding, interpreting and
anticipating the human personality are strewn with the
spirits of many psychologists and psychiatrists, so the
problem-solving manager is recommended to concentrate
on the more likely success approaches: initially, the
observation of overt behaviour, the situation surrounding
the event and the consequent observable effects.

Within this approach awareness and observation are of paramount importance. However, the expression 'I see' covers a range of methods which might be employed.

The simplest, though not necessarily the most effective approach, is to be aware and to know at first hand what is going on. The GOYA principle has already been discussed and it is only by getting off the managerial seat to see what the workers are actually doing that direct evidence will be to hand. There are people with a naturally keen awareness who can take in a mass of visible data at a glance and who have an ability to see a problem with an uncanny directness. I have worked in an organization which had a system of occasional inspection by a special team of investigators. Most of the investigators worked through the material to be examined in a thorough, methodical way and if errors had been made they would eventually come to light. But one inspector had this uncanny ability of taking a bundle of documents and going immediately to the one with an error. Unfortunately for the mass of mere mortals the more laborious, methodical approach must be the road to travel and, as suggested by the word 'methodical', some system must be employed.

STAGE 2   WHAT IS HAPPENING?

Once we have identified, however tentatively or even intuitively that a problem exists, we must define as widely and as specifically as possible its extent and nature. This will require observation of some form, depending on its complexity.

Simple watching of the operation or the person in action may be all that is necessary to identify the problem, the specific event which is causing it and any other relevant factors. On one occasion a machine operation was being interrupted frequently by the safety cut-off. The machine had been examined and passed 100 per cent by the maintenance fitter, but the fault continued. I watched the operator for five minutes during which time the machine failed twice. However, I noticed that the machine stopped on both occasions when the operator leaned over to make a regular adjustment. On the third occasion I noted that as he leaned across his shoulder touched a part which brought the safety action into operation. Why had this not happened previously? The present operator was left-handed and it was discovered that his predecessors had all been right-handed. Consequently they leaned over the machine at a different angle and did not trigger the safety-guard. Would that all problems were as simple as that to solve!

The above observation could be described as a simple form of activity analysis. If we extend this technique to more complex activities, results of a similar nature can be obtained to pinpoint the specific problem. In essence, activity analysis means regular and specific observation recording the elements of the activity and the differences from the norm, thus identifying the problem event.

If we have, for example, identified a problem in stage 1 which involves one worker only, but it is not evident in similar workers performing the same duty, ideally the observation will be in two stages. The first stage will be observing and recording the activities and behaviour of a worker with no problems, and analysing these observations on the basis of, let us say, critical activities and behaviours. We are producing a detailed and specific job profile against which other profiles can be measured.

The second stage of the analysis is to perform an identical activity sampling on the suspected problem performer in order to obtain a discrete profile for comparison with the norm. In most cases this should be sufficient to pinpoint the problem.

In practice, the manager may have to perform the activity analysis rather than enjoy the luxury of having a specialist department or organization to do it for him. In such cases, instead of carrying out a formal first stage, the manager will probably rely on his own knowledge to set the norm of effective and efficient working. He will then compare the problem events with the known factors to identify where the problem might lie. This pragmatic approach is readily acceptable provided that the manager is really in a position to know the job as well as he thinks he does.

Whatever the fullness or otherwise of the approach, the steps are similar and involve all or most of the following:

1   An examination of the job description and any clarification necessary of doubtful areas
2   Observation and analysis of the job performance of a known successful performer
3   Observation and analysis of the job performance of the problem performer
4   Comparison of the two profiles and pinpointing of the problem areas.

It is perhaps at stage 2 above and certainly at stage 3 that ethical questions may emerge. If the people being observed are not aware of the activity, ethics may suggest that what is occurring is immoral spying and interference with personal liberties and human rights. On the other hand, if the people concerned are made aware of the observation, this awareness may contaminate the analysis. Certainly as far as the effective person is concerned, there should be full discussion and agreement before any observation. In the case of the problem person the decision is far from clear, but knowledge of being observed may completely negate any normal (i.e. problem) behaviour. If the observer is clearly evident and visible one compromise may be to say that it is the job which is being analysed.

If either or both subjects, the effective worker and the problem worker, are aware that they are being observed, at least two effects may result:

1   The workers may perform unnaturally, ensuring as far as possible that they are following the 'book' with the work being done as well or better than if there had been no observer
2   Unnaturally perfect performance occurs over an initial period only during which the performer is super-aware of the observation. However, as the individual becomes immersed in the work, the presence of the observer may be forgotten. At such a stage the

performer returns to normal levels of work perhaps for a sufficiently long period for the errors to occur.

The process of observation can be simplified by the use of basic recording and analytical tools. For the straight-forward task a simple job content observation sheet can be supplied to the observer, the sheet having been constructed from the detailed job profile description. The observer watches the worker and logs each time an aspect of the work is performed, perhaps also timing both the occurrence and its duration. At the end of the observational period the scoring is analysed in terms of the frequency of each event, its duration, perhaps at what part of the day or shift, and its success and so on.

Behaviour observation

The observation of behaviour requires a different form of analytical instrument and the most useful which I have found is Behaviour Analysis, an interaction analysis developed by Neil Rackham, Peter Honey and others.

Behaviour observation, however, is similar in many ways to process observation since it is also the analysis of someone performing an activity. But in this case we are more interested in the human behaviour patterns than the practical aspects of the job. Process observation has its base in a fairly regular, mechanical process; behaviour observation relates to what a person says, how they say it or how they express thoughts through non-verbal communication. Consequently, the prime requirement of behaviour analysis is the selection of the behaviour categories, observation of the incidence of these behaviours and a recording of this incidence so that an eventual analysis of frequency can be made. The selection of the behaviour categories should be relatively simple following the initial analysis of the job description, but whereas many jobs need to be performed in one way, human interactions do not follow such a logical path.

The first decision on which behaviours to observe will be based on the job description guidelines and the skill of the practitioner in performing behaviour observation. The latter task is relatively easy where the requirement is to record the behaviours of one person only. It is quite different when observation is being made of a group of people.

Previous chapters have described some of the human behaviours encountered which will form a basis for the category selection. They are as follows:

Closed questions
Multiple questions
Multiple choice questions
Leading questions
Open questions
Testing understanding
Inviting
Reflecting
Proposing
Suggesting
Building
Giving information, opinions, views, feelings
Seeking information, opinions, views, feelings, ideas
Summarizing
Supporting/agreeing
Disagreeing
Attacking
Blocking
Open
Interrupting.

It may be necessary to subdivide some of these categories, e.g. proposing may have several contextual variations, or it may be advisable to exclude some from the list. One helpful experience which might give a clue to the vital behaviours for observation is the analysis of the behaviour of the effective performer. A number of studies have already been made to determine effective behaviour patterns in meetings, negotiations and appraisal interviews and, although the sample is small, the effective performer

gives at least some guide to the behaviours which are more
likely to be successful.

Again, in the same way that a format can be developed
for the process observation, the activities of a behaviour
analysis can also be logged as they occur. A typical
example, developed by the author for analysing appraisal
interviews, is shown in Figure 7.1. This type of scoring
sheet can be modified easily to suit the situation and can be
varied to include either verbal or non-verbal behaviour, or,
if the observer is sufficiently skilled, a combination of both.

	Inter-viewer	Inter-viewee	TOTAL
Suggesting/proposing			
Open questions			
Closed questions			
Multiple questions			
Leading questions			
Reflecting			
Giving information			
Disagreeing without reasons			
Disagreeing with reasons			
Testing understanding			
Summarizing			
Supporting			
Open			
Attacking/blocking			
Interrupting			
TOTALS			

Figure 7.1   Behaviour observation form

When this type of behaviour observation form is used, each
time the problem person makes a contribution, whether it
is verbal or non-verbal depending on the nature of the

analysis, the event is logged as a mark on the analysis sheet against the relevant category. It may also be valuable to record the contributions made by any other person in the interaction to obtain a full behavioural picture of the event.

At the end of the observation the scorings are analysed and compared with the effective behaviour pattern, upon which analysis a significant variation might be evident.

As an example we can use the case of the hotel receptionist who was felt to be a problem. She seemed not to be working as efficiently and perhaps not as hard as her colleagues, but mostly these were subjective feelings with no objective evidence. The investigator ensured that he had a complete grasp of the requirements of the job (so that she was not judged unfairly) by studying the job description and job profile. He also talked to some of the other receptionists to obtain a more personal assessment of the nature of the job and its requirements. In these conversations he also included the 'problem' worker so that there was no suggestion that she had been 'left out' and also from the viewpoint that she might disclose something unwittingly – she didn't.

An analysis was performed on two receptionists who had been assessed by the management as fully efficient and effective. The analysis included an activity log of the duties performed:

1 Process booking of accommodation by letter
2 Process booking of accommodation by telephone
3 Process booking of accommodation in person
4 Preparation of customer's bill
5 Modification of bill on presentation – additions etc.

It also included a verbal behaviour analysis:

6 . Amount of seeking information, needs, requirements
7 Clarification of information given by customer
8 Giving information in response to customer query

And a non-verbal behaviour analysis:

9 Amount of smiling at customer

10   Percentage of looking at customer
11   Use of head nods and shakes (any variation with cultures)
12   Amount of touching.

The subjects were observed on a number of occasions in order to produce patterns rather than isolated incident periods, and to ensure reasonable accuracy of observation, and a number of items of interest emerged. Firstly it was seen from the behaviour analyses that there were few problems in this area. The receptionist asked the relevant questions at the appropriate times; gave all the necessary information either when or before being asked; smiled to a reasonable extent; used but did not over-use the customer's name etc. However, when the activity logging was examined, it was found that there was an area in which she did far less work than any of the other receptionists and that she excused herself from these areas of work by asking other receptionists to perform them, saying that she was busy in some other way, or had an absenting mission to perform.

Attention was then concentrated on this activity. It emerged that in every case the customer was coming to settle the hotel account. Other indications existed which showed that the receptionist had no mathematical or accounting problems. She was quite capable of handling cash and constructing accounts and bills with relative ease.

It was obviously necessary to investigate this behaviour further, for although the problem was evident – avoidance of bill-paying customers – and the consequences were known – progressively worse relationships with colleagues and a lowering of personal work load – the reason was still not in sight. An obvious solution might be to move her to work which avoided contact with outgoing customers, but this was not desirable for a number of reasons, the principal one being that she was such a good personal receptionist in all other ways. It had also come to light, from discussions with the management, that this problem behaviour was a change from a satisfactory previous situation.

It was decided to interview the receptionist in order to try and pinpoint the problem further and identify the reasons. The interview would be conducted as part of the organization's normal appraisal system so as not to upset the interviewee unduly. In the structural terms of such an interview, it would be basically an appraisal interview but with additional problem-solving objectives and with the possibility that counselling might become necessary. In this particular case the pinpointing stage 2 would be prefaced by a brief following stage.

STAGE 3 DEFINITION OF THE DESIRED SITUATION

Before any positive action is taken find a remedy, the problem having been defined as accurately as possible, the objectives for the next activity must be decided. In the majority of cases these objectives will be to resolve the problem in terms of maintaining the job description. There will be occasions when perhaps the return to the full job requirement may need to be modified, possibly with the acceptance of a lower level of work. But this must be a conscious decision rather than an emotional acceptance of a situation. It must also be borne in mind that resolution of the problem may fail and in such cases some forethought must be given to subsequent more drastic solutions such as job movement, relocation or dismissal.

In the case of the hotel receptionist, the stage 3 decision had been made that the present situation could not continue and further attempts had to be made to identify the problem and achieve a solution. If this were not possible, discipline procedures would have to be instituted leading to, if unsuccessful, an offer of a lower-level, less demanding job or discharge.

The act of commencing an interview with the receptionist as described earlier starts in stage 2, develops through stage 3 and could develop into the stage 4 activity of deciding an action.

STAGE 4   DECISIONS ON ACTION

In the case of the hotel receptionist, the interview will start naturally with a discussion of the individual's work and her reaction to it. In time it is hoped this will lead to her views on problem areas, her acceptance of the problem and, once emerged, further information about how she saw the problem.

In the event she disclosed that she was now terrified of having to modify bills when queried by the customer and she had experienced two aggravated interactions of this nature. Further discussion revealed that modification of a bill required a process using a recently added part of the accounts machine located for use by the receptionists. When the new facility had been added she had been on holiday and on her return nobody had passed on the training everybody else had received. She had tried on one or two occasions to do it herself, but the processes were complex and she had not been successful. Unfortunately a variety of factors had prevented her from seeking help so she had evolved a system of avoiding the problem. She had been aware of the effect she was having on her colleagues and was on the point of giving notice to leave.

There seemed to be one solution in this case. It was readily agreed that, as she did not want to leave, she should receive special training in the use of the new facility. She was concerned that she might appear foolish if the training happened in front of her colleagues, so arrangements were made for her to receive the training at the machine supplier's premises. The possibility of using another hotel for training was discussed but rejected on the grounds that there might be some interchange of comments between the hotels and she might be embarrassed.

Not all cases will be resolved as smoothly and relatively easily as this one, but the following guidelines will assist the process:

- Pinpoint the problem as far as possible by direct observation
- Pinpoint further by an interaction with the person

concerned
- Do not jump to conclusions before all available evidence is gathered
- Seek a number of possible solutions whenever this is relevant
- Discuss the various options and agree the most acceptable to both parties
- Once decided, take action.

In the case of the receptionist, the eventual solution required the modification of the individual. But in some instances the variation will require a modification of the job itself. Investigation may show that the problem lies in the job, the specification of the job, the way in which it has been presented, the instructions or briefing for the performance of the job, and so on. Consequently the solution to the problem performance may be in the job or its environment rather than in the individual.

BEHAVIOURAL PROBLEMS

So many of the problems which arise at work (and, indeed, throughout life) are based on behaviour between people. These problems may be caused by either words or deeds, with an emphasis towards the former, as deeds are but physical entities which are usually obvious in their overt practice. But words are subject to a variety of interpretations and they can so often be the triggers of emotive reactions.

Of course, these reactions are what make human life so interesting in its unpredictability – or at least we assume this unpredictability and in many cases are correct. However, there is a large part of human behaviour which has a reasonable degree of predictability and if we are to utilize behaviour to the full in our avoidance and solution of problems, any possibility of predictability must be seized.

One of the observers of human behaviour who has considered the likelihoods of these behaviours is Peter

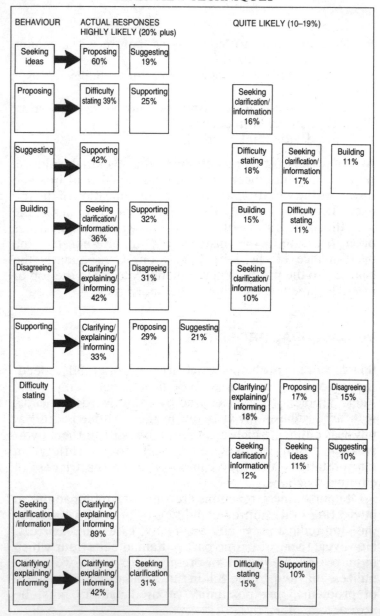

Figure 7.2 **Shaping behaviour – how the behaviours function**

Honey. In several hundred interactions which he observed he analysed the behaviours not only by identifying and logging the categories of the contributions, but also the sequential reactions of the behaviours. From these studies he identified the percentage likelihood response rates to a number of behaviours. His chart summarizing these findings is reproduced in Figure 7.2.

The findings suggest the likely response rate to behaviours initiated by an individual. For example, if the trigger behaviour is 'Seeking ideas', the percentage likelihood response rate is 60 per cent Proposing and 19 per cent Suggesting, both positive initiating behaviours. This appears to be a commonsense response, but on so many occasions when a task is to be performed and ideas are necessary, the question is not in fact asked, probably in the hope (subconscious) that proposals will emerge. Quite often they do, but on a large number of occasions nothing or other things happen. The behavioural message is that if you want ideas to emerge, ask directly for them and there is a very strong likelihood that you will receive them.

On the other hand if the trigger behaviour is that of 'Difficulty stating', this behaviour can be received in so many ways that almost any response is possible and the difficulty stater must be prepared for this. If the initiator is not a behaviourally aware person, this completely unpredictable response can cause all sorts of problems coming as it does 'out of the blue'.

Knowledge of and skill in the use of these behavioural likelihoods can help to make interactions more pleasant and effective. A full awareness of behaviours and reactions in the early stages may result in some stiff and awkward moments, but with practice, like any new technique, the use of behaviours will become almost second nature. Some individuals react against this type of approach, accusing the method of encouraging deviousness and the manipulation of people. In many ways there is no rebuttal to these accusations other than the justification that if behaviours are allowed to take their own course, much more is likely to go wrong. The 'commonsense' approach has probably been the cause of more interactive problems at all levels than any other factor. People problems are the most difficult to solve, but they can produce really effective results.

8 Planning the interview

We have now considered many of the basic elements of the interview – the physical aspects, the various viewpoints which can be held by different people, the structuring of an interview, questioning and other interaction behaviours, listening and the levels of interviewing. When these are mastered the next step is to bring them all together in preparation for the interview. The military has always found that the time spent on reconnaissance before an attack is well spent, with a value greater in proportion than the actual attack time. So with the interview. Even with the best techniques available, there is a greater likelihood of something going wrong if the event has had little or no planning. Many managers and supervisors believe that either

- interviewers are born, not made, and that they themselves were born this way
- interviewing is just common sense and that this is a commodity of which they have a considerable supply
- whatever happens during the interview, they can cope with it.

The pathway of interviewing is littered with the debris of events based on these attitudes. There *are* people born with natural interviewing skills, there *are* people endowed with a massive dose of common sense and there *are* people who are positively reactive to immediate events. But the majority of those who are called upon to interview are less gifted and must rely principally on learned skills to avoid frequent disaster. It is for this majority that a full planning approach can be of considerable help. No amount of planning can ensure that every eventuality is considered, but at the very least the process ensures coverage of the most likely issues. This is one of the strengths of planning: once you sit down to think about what could happen, a number of other possible issues come to mind which would otherwise not have emerged in a superficial consideration or if not considered at all.

Another important advantage of planning is that some provision can be made if the interviewee diverges from the path which was intended by the interviewer. The interviewer can be lulled into a false sense of security in the early stages of the interview if everything seems to be going well. But suddenly the interview can take a completely unexpected turn as a result of a change of direction by the interviewee: the consequence can often be complete confusion on the part of the interviewer who is totally unprepared for this. If the event has been planned, even if the interview does not follow the interviewer's script, all that is usually necessary is a modification of the original plan rather than a complete rethink on the spot. This is a much less traumatic experience for the interviewer who can often, quickly, bring the event back to the intended route.

The process of planning the interview can be described in a structured manner by utilizing a logical model. This model will be described in seven stages:

1   The *issue review* in which the reasons for holding the interview are analysed from the viewpoints of both the interviewer *and* the interviewee.
2   A determination of the *aims* of the interview, leading to more specific
3   *Objectives* which are the measures of the achievement of the interview.
4   In order to assess the achievement of these objectives, *key success factors* have to be identified which can be matched against the objectives following the interview.
5   There is very little use in determining *what* has to be done if *how* it is to be done is not considered, so the

methods to be used must form part of the process.

6 The key to any interaction with people is the use of appropriate *behaviours*. These can be planned in the same way as structure and processes.

7 Finally, very little is learned if what has happened in the interview is not *reviewed* following the event. Learning is a cyclical process and every incident in which we become involved is an opportunity for learning. A post-event assessment is essential both to review success or otherwise and also to plan further action.

ISSUE REVIEW

As mentioned earlier, one of the advantages of planning the event is that issues and potential problems can be considered beforehand. This is obviously preferable to dealing with them 'off the top of the head' as they emerge during the event. Not only are the planner's views exposed for careful thought, but also any issues and attitudes of the other person which are not necessarily in agreement with the planner. In fact it may be desirable to consider deliberately the possible contrasting views of the other person rather than just our own.

This approach can be described as the 'issue review'. We start by considering the issues we intend to raise, and in so doing we prioritize them, to rehearse the ways in which they should be raised, and even to decide whether they should be raised at all. By writing them down their reality is confirmed and their importance determined. Often issues which appear enormous when contained in our mind, shrink considerably in importance and value when committed to paper. Stage 1 of this process is shown in Figure 8.1.

Once identified the issues are examined to determine to what extent they will be problems in the interview and could produce conflict, or will be readily accepted or agreed by the other. The difference can be identified in some way personal to the planner – √ and X, * and o, + and –, etc. Those which are clearly identified as not presenting any problem will need little further

---

My interview issues

1   To consider and ensure that he is aware of my knowledge of his actions

2   To obtain any further information from him

3   To reprimand him

Figure 8.1   Issue review – stage 1

consideration, but those annotated with, for example, x, o or – are thus flagged for further thought.

Consider the problem areas identified.

- Is it necessary to raise them?
- Why will the other person reject them?
- Will all of the issue be rejected or only part?
- Which will be the best way to present the issue?
- What words should be used?
- What should be done if he . . . ? etc.

If this process is followed, the interview planner should be mentally prepared for each issue as far as possible within the natural constraints. The principal constraint is the attempt to put oneself in the mind of the other person.

Previous knowledge may help, but even when the two people are familiar to each other, they may be in a situation together which neither has experienced before. In such a case, historical knowledge of reactions may be of little use. In spite of such constraints, the very act of considering the situation will help, even by producing realization that the possible reaction is not known. Consequently it will be necessary to consider alternative approaches. So the issue review will be developed as Figure 8.2.

In-depth consideration of issue 3 shows that part would be accepted and part rejected. Further consideration suggests that the cause of action most likely to succeed would be to split it into two separate issues and treat them accordingly.

My interview issues

1   Issue .....
     Likely reaction ✓
     Action .....

2   Issue .....
     Likely reaction ✗
     Action a ..... or
            b .....

3   Issue .....
     Likely reaction: part ✓ part ✗
     Action: divide the issue into two parts 3a and 3b

3a   Issue .....
     Likely reaction ✓
     Action .....

3b   Issue .....
     Likely reaction ✗
     Action .....

Figure 8.2 Issue review – stage 2

A start has been made on the difficult approach of considering the possible reaction of the interviewee to the issues. But the interviewee may also have some issues which are additional to or different from those of the interviewer. The same process is then followed again, but looking at the interaction from the other person's point of view – his likely issues, the interviewer's attitude to them and the likely action of the interviewer to resolve any disagreement. The complete issue review is summarized in Figure 8.3.

There is no guarantee that, having followed this approach, all the outcomes will be identified and the actions will be successful, but it is considerably better than

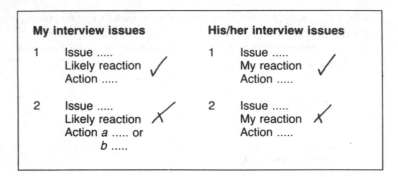

Figure 8.3   Issue review – stage 3

doing nothing. It can conceivably anticipate most, if not all, of the potential problems; and it will certainly prepare the interviewer for issues which would not normally have been raised; and it gives the opportunity for options to be considered and weighed and, within the constraints, decisions made.

PLANNING

The issue review forms only one part of the planning process and, although methods are considered, it concentrates principally on the task to be achieved. But an interview consists of both the task to be performed and the process by which it is to be achieved. Consequently we need to consider both these aspects, bearing in mind that there is another person involved – a person with a personality and behaviour of their own who will react to our personality and behaviour, whether this is in or out of step with the task. It is impossible to plan for every eventuality, but at least we are ensuring a greater likelihood of success.

Planning an interview is little different from planning any other task, and it is important to be aware of the vagaries of the other person, an individual in his own right. Above all, we should be aware of the behaviours involved in the interaction.

The recommended planning model is one which I use myself, particularly when taking part in important interactions. As well as following the model, it is essential to write down the plan rather than try to retain it mentally. When we are considering the outcome of an event, the mind can conveniently forget certain parts of what we intended to do, consciously or subconsciously. If it is written down beforehand we cannot disclaim our original intentions. The model is summarized in Figure 8.4.

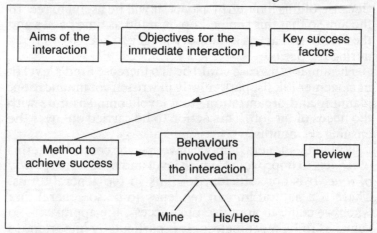

Figure 8.4   Interaction planning model

To demonstrate the process let us imagine a member of staff who is in need of development, both remedial and long-term. It is considered that a project could help him overcome his problems of planning and organization, and the eventual write-up of the project will aid the improvement of his written skills. He is aware that he has not yet reached the desired level of performance and he also knows that you are aware of the shortcomings. You have asked to see him tomorrow to discuss his progress and his future and have suggested that you might discuss a particular project for him to attempt. He is normally a reasonable young man and you have no reason to believe he will be difficult.

AIMS OF THE INTERACTION

It is rare that an interaction is a unique occurrence, with no bearing on any other activities. In the case we are considering there is no doubt that the interaction planned for the morrow will be part of a series of subsequent meetings over a period of time. This series will be intended to achieve more than that of the initial meeting only. Because of this long-term aspect, it will be useful to record the aim so that this can be kept in mind as time passes and the record will act as a memory jogger to keep us on track during the period.

The aim for this case could be 'To increase Fred's level of management skills, particularly in written communication, planning and organization, to a level commensurate with the needs of his job. This action to be carried out over the ensuing six months.'

Within this general aim we have specific controls in terms of *what* is to improve, to *which* level and over which *period of time*. It is not sufficient to think in too general terms. There is a natural human tendency to be so general that when we come to appraise our success, the appraisal is so vague as to be meaningless. It is particularly important to state the time constraint as this can help ensure that we take action rather than procrastinate.

OBJECTIVES FOR THE IMMEDIATE INTERACTION

The next stage is to consider the specific, immediate objectives for the interaction we are to have tomorrow with Fred. The objectives are the determination of what we intend to have achieved by the end of the interview. Naturally they will depend on the time we shall have available and also, from what we know of Fred and his likely reactions, the extent to which we are likely to move in the time. If we know that because our knowledge of Fred is limited we cannot estimate his likely reaction, or we know that he will take up a difficult attitude, our objectives will probably be more restricted.

The objectives must be couched, and written for the same reasons as cited above, in positive behavioural terms and must represent a realistic assessment of the desired and most likely outcome. If possible, they should be stated in more specific terms than those of the aims, so that there can be no subsequent doubt in our mind that we have either succeeded or failed.

Because we feel that we know Fred well and feel fairly sure of his likely reaction, possible objectives for the first interaction might be:

1   To obtain Fred's agreement that development is necessary in his case
2   To agree with Fred that the most appropriate action would be for him to take charge of project X
3   To determine and agree the main steps in the project
4   To arrange the action, the date and the time for the next meeting
5   To arrange provisionally a programme of review meetings
6   To achieve this in a period of no longer than 1½ hours.

Underpinning these objectives is the intention that all will be achieved not only with Fred's agreement, but also that Fred himself will be an active agent in the planning. The principal reasoning behind this approach will include:

• the problem is Fred's and he should therefore be active in the solution
• Fred's commitment is more likely if he is instrumental in proposing the various actions.

KEY SUCCESS FACTORS

Once the interaction has been completed we should be able to quantify the extent of its success. This entails the assessment of the outcome of each of the set objectives. In order to do this we need a mechanism to measure the level of this success. When considering the setting of objectives we might ask 'What do we hope to achieve by the end of the interview?'. After the interaction we have to ask 'Have we achieved our objectives and to what extent?'. To answer this question we must have a set of factors or indicators to demonstrate this success: 'How do we know that we have achieved this success?'.

The first objective was 'to obtain agreement with Fred that development is necessary in his case'. A key success factor could be that by the end of the interaction Fred will have volunteered the statement that he needs to and wants to develop. If this has occurred, we can be fairly confident that the objective has been achieved, but if the agreement is not actually stated we cannot be certain of Fred's real acceptance.

A second key success factor would again be Fred's overt agreement without qualification to undertake the project as part of his development. In order to satisfy the commitment criterion, we must end up with a plan for the main steps in the project and also the commitment that 'Fred proposes at least 50 per cent of the action steps'. By doing this we also have further confirmation of his agreement both to the project and his development.

Another key success factor relates to the arrangement for the next meeting linked with a series of review meetings. It is not sufficient for the interviewer to suggest these actions, much better for most of it to come from the interviewee. Again, if this occurs we can be reasonably certain that there is commitment and the interviewee has been fully involved in the process.

Finally, if the meeting was contained with 1½ hours, this is a further key success factor, but if a longer period of time is taken, this objective has not been achieved and the interviewer has stolen time from an activity in which he should have been engaged.

These key success factors (KSFs) form the basis for an internal dialogue which the interviewer might have with himself to determine the satisfaction of the objectives. It is at this stage that the advantages of writing down all aspects of the plan become apparent. It is only too easy to forget some parts of the objectives and key success factors if they have been recorded mentally only, and much more difficult to avoid self-confrontation if they have been written down.

Consideration of the KSFs can be useful in two areas – the task itself and the process, the two factors which should be taken into account in the pursuance of any activity. The KSFs relate principally to the task: what was achieved, to what extent it was achieved, on which parts agreements were reached, the type and extent of agreement, and so on. Again, as a self-discipline and regulator of post-interview rationalization, it is useful to have a similar set of questions written down which can be used as an inquisition.

Consideration of the success of the process is related to a later stage in the planning, which is concerned with the behaviours to be used in the interaction. This is the stage which is rarely given much attention when an interaction is being planned, consideration being concentrated on structure. But the pre-planning of behaviour, as far as possible, is probably more important than any other aspect since it is ultimately on the behavioural interaction between the participants that the interview may succeed or fail.

METHODS TO ACHIEVE SUCCESS

Before we examine behaviour, it may be useful to consider the structure and approach for the interview. Decisions on these aspects will certainly revolve around what we know of the interviewee, his attitudes and his likely reaction to our approaches. The best way to approach some people, and we have to be absolutely certain about this, is in a direct authoritative, almost autocratic manner; with others we must take a more gentle, participative approach; with others there must be a degree of flattery; and so on. Remember, however, that the person we are inter-viewing may not be at that time the same as he 'always' is. Quiet, even-tempered Bill who is always open to reasonable argument, may not be on this occasion and the apparent reversal of behaviour may take us unawares. This change may be due to stress, illness, or a sequence of events, so although we may have to start the interaction from the only base of which we are aware, we shall have to be prepared to modify our approach.

Underpinning the whole interview is the structure which we *intend* to follow, bearing in mind any modification if the occasion demands it. An early statement by the interviewee may have a significant effect on the progress of the interview. Take it as soon as it arises.

The structure of the interview relates to its nature and the many different structures will be considered later. Although there will be differences, in many cases these will be degrees of difference rather than major variations. For example, in a job appraisal interview the introductory stage will probably take a little longer than, say, in a grievance interview in which the introductory part will be virtually non-existent. Bearing these variations in mind, the *normal* structure of an interview is likely to be as follows:

1 Introductory stage
2 Investigatory or information gathering stage
3 Generation of possible solutions
4 Consideration of possible solutions
5 Decision-making stage
6 Concluding or summarizing stage.

The difference between the interview types will determine the variation between the same stage in different interviews. Similarly, the behaviours for different interviews will emerge in different ways, governed by the appropriateness of the situation.

INTERACTIVE BEHAVIOUR PLANNING

In an interaction between two people there are two sets of behaviour – that of the interviewer and of the interviewee. Two common reactions are found when behaviour planning is introduced. The interviewer is likely to say when it is suggested that he might wish to plan his behaviour: 'Oh, it'll be alright. I'll play it by ear!' This statement by interviewers has caused more distress for both themselves and the interviewees than any other. Few of us have the skill to do this naturally in every situation and where problem interviews arise, the resultant lack of preparation causes at best a hiatus with the interviewer not knowing what to say next, or at worst a blow-up between the two parties. What the interviewer is really saying when he makes this statement is that he will do exactly what he wants to do whether or not this upsets the other person.

Similar problems can arise when it is suggested to the interviewer that he might consider the behaviour possibilities of the interviewee before commencing the, what must be, unknown voyage. Sometimes an approach to this is made, as suggested earlier when the interviewer might contemplate the likely attitude of the interviewee – but little more than that. Otherwise the interviewer might be heard to say 'How on earth do I know what he's likely to say?' or 'I'll deal with his reaction as it comes'. Again what the interviewer is really saying is 'I'll do what I want to do!' It is agreed that the words the interviewee might say are not known, but if the interviewer has any behavioural skill at all, what the interviewee says will be the direct consequence of the stimulus given by the interviewer. In very simplistic terms, if the interviewer asks a question, the most likely response will be some information given by the interviewee. Within these likelihoods of stimulus and response lie the different paths of the interview.

By using the case study described earlier we can plot a likely behavioural progress of the interview and plan not only the behaviours but their probable sequence.

Let us look first at the behaviours we want the interviewee to exhibit. We shall want him to describe to us his feelings, views and opinions on how he thinks he is or is not developing. The sequence is as follows:

1 *Give information, feelings, views or opinions.* Subsequently, following a discussion about this situation, let us assume that he accepts his non-development. However, he may wish to question us on

our views of his progress, so we shall find that he will probably

2 *Seek information, views, opinions etc.* What we will then be looking for is for him to

3 *Propose* a course of action to remedy the situation or at least some initial ideas for this course of action. Because one of our objectives was concerned with his agreement to perform a project, we shall want him then to

4 *Support* any proposals or suggestions we might make and then for him to

5 *Propose* possible ways in which the steps of the project can be taken. It may be necessary for us to receive from him further

6 *Support* or if he cannot do this, to

7 *Disagree* stating his reasons fully and without being asked. Once the plan has been agreed we are looking to him to

8 *Propose* (*a*) a series of review meetings; (*b*) the next meeting and its agenda.

The format of this desired behaviour will encourage him to put forward ideas on the basis suggested earlier, that the more involved he is in the creation of the plan, the more committed he will be to it. Above all we want the interviewee to talk rather than be a passive listener and accepter of our views. We do not want him to

● be obstructive and baldly and bluntly disagree
● be over-emotive and defend his position by attacking
● make non-relevant comments or facetious remarks of a blocking nature
● interrupt, since this will suggest he is not listening when we are talking.

In summary, the behaviours we want from him are principally: giving information, seeking information, proposing, supporting and disagreeing (but only with reasons).

How are we, the interviewers, to achieve these desired behaviours? Principally by utilizing the variation in our own behaviours. Consequently the behaviours we will exhibit will follow a pattern of:

1 *Giving information* – setting the scene for the interaction
2 *Seeking information* – the information he has, his views, opinions etc. (his 1)
3 *Giving information* – responding to his seeking our views on the situation (his 2)
4 *Seeking ideas* – asking him how we can remedy the situation and looking for a proposal from him (his 3)
5 *Suggesting or building* – depending on his proposal we might build on this so that a composite idea becomes the basis for the project. However, if our seeking of ideas fails to produce a proposal, we shall suggest the project. By the fact that we are suggesting, rather than the more prescriptive proposing, we are looking for his support (his 4)
6 *Seeking ideas* – following his assumed support for our suggestion we then want him to propose in detail (his 5)
7 *Supporting or building* – this behaviour set will depend on the nature of the ideas coming from him in his behaviour 5. We hope that his ideas will allow us to support him or if necessary to build. However, we may need to
8 *Disagree with reasons*. Whichever behaviour we utilize in our 7 or 8, we are trying to ensure that he will support or disagree with reasons (his 6 or 7).

This approach will continue until the plans for the project are complete, with repetitions of our 5, 7 or 8. Then we would

9 *Summarize* – in which we are seeking his agreement/ support.

The process would be continued by moving on to the review procedure in which we would again

10 *Seek ideas* – looking to his proposing response (his 8) which we shall, if possible

11 *Support.*

When all agreements are made we would once more, and finally,

12 *Summarize.*

This plan has a built-in flexibility in case he does not respond to our seeking his ideas in our behaviour 4. Possibly he may respond that he has no ideas to put forward. As suggested against our 5, if this negative response is the result, we could make an initial suggestion, but following his response we could return to our plan at 4. Because we have managed to start him on stating some views, there is a greater likelihood that he will be encouraged to put forward some ideas of his own once the process has started.

The principle of this planning concept is that it is easier to modify an existing plan while the action is under way, rather than, without a plan, to decide off the top of one's head what to do – not an easy process.

In order to complete the behaviour plan, we must avoid the following behaviours:

- interrupting
- blocking
- attacking
- disagreeing (without giving reasons)
- not listening and, if we can avoid it,
- proposing – we should suggest.

REVIEW

Once the interaction is complete we must review the event, looking particularly at the key success factors to assess whether or not the objectives have been achieved. Since we have written these down, assessment should be relatively simple, merely a checking of the KSFs against what happened in the interview. If all the KSFs were achieved, the objectives will have been satisfied, but if some have not then the interaction cannot have been a complete success.

But the value of assessing the effects of the interview does not rest only in the assessment of the success or otherwise of the interview itself. The interview can be used as a learning event from which lessons can be taken for future interactions. It is rarely that we take the opportunity of treating an experience as a learning process, but a logical approach will ensure that we extract the maximum learning benefit.

The process starts naturally with our involvement in the interview itself, our participation as the interviewer. If the end of the interview were to be the end of the process, little learning would ensue. In order to obtain some benefit from the experience, a follow-up action is essential rather than moving onto the next event, whatever this might be. Begin by reflecting on the experience and its implications, an approach already discussed when we looked at the key result factors. The initial reflection is about the task and we need answers to such questions as 'Were the objectives achieved? Was it a good interview? Did the other person and I feel good at the end of the event? What actually happened during the event?'

Self-questioning at this level will produce factual or semi-factual answers and although these will tell us *what* happened, we need to probe deeper for real learning. The aspects of behaviour and their results will be valuable in this deeper-level probing – the analysis stage, which requires answers to the following questions: 'Did I use all the behaviours I had planned to use? If yes, what reactions did they produce? If not, why not and what were the resultant reactions? Did I use any behaviours I had not intended to use? If so, what reactions did they produce? Which behaviours did the other person use? How did I react to these?' And to take the self-questioning to level 4: 'How did I feel when he said/did that?'

As a result of asking questions such as these, particularly and 'how' and 'why' questions, and in effect conducting an analytical self-dialogue, a considerable amount of data can be produced which should confirm why the process of the interview either helped or hindered the event.

Again, if the learning process stops at this point and no

practical use is made of it, the mental processes used have been a waste of time. But if we carry our thought processes through to the planning stage, the store of data and learning can be considered in other situations: 'Would I use the same method/behaviours/reactions with Mary? If not, why not? What modifications would I make? How do I think she would feel if x happened as it did with Bill?' And so on.

The expectation or hope is that each event becomes a learning situation and if we extract the maximum amount of learning from each event and consider its future use, we shall build up a data bank of learned experience. Consequently, following interactions are more likely to succeed when the previous learning is applied. By treating each event in isolation we ignore

- basic interviewing requirements
- variant viewpoints
- interview structures
- questioning techniques
- interview behaviours
- levels of interviewing
- interaction planning.

A recipe for failure.

9 Acquiring the skills

Although some interviewers are born with all the natural skills which enable them to conduct an efficient and effective interaction, the majority have limited skill only which needs to be supplemented. How is the caring manager or supervisor to acquire the extensive range of skills described in this book? Whenever training is mentioned the usual immediate thought is 'Is there a training course which I can attend?'. Although there are many relevant and effective training courses available it is not absolutely necessary to attend them; there are many suitable alternatives.

One of the disadvantages of training courses about dealing with people is that the 'real' interactions occur back at work. An effective training course may include lots of practical, experiential activities which attempt to replicate the situation 'back at the ranch', and on many occasions emotions, feelings, attitudes and reactions may make the practice interview real for the participants. But after the event it is still seen as an artificial simulation when related to the interviews in which the participants will become involved: real subordinates in real situations. Although there has been useful practice, the crunch will come when a member of staff is sitting in front of you and you have to reprimand him without losing a basically good worker. If you make a mess of the interview you cannot say (as on a training course): 'Hang on, let me try that again!'. Of course, if the training has been skilled and has offered sufficient practice with appraisal you should not make any big errors in your first real interview, provided that you put into practice what you have learned.

The most straightforward learning step is the realization that there are (a) different types of interaction and (b) different methods of approaching them. One relatively simple method, for some people, is to read a book such as the one you now have in your hand. A book of this nature sets out to provide, remind or confirm the basic knowledge about interactions. But what it can never do is teach you how to interview – only actual experience of interviewing in a variety of situations will ever do this. However, you must learn the various avenues available, how to structure the different types of interview and how to use behaviours to achieve your objectives. A book is one way of achieving this knowledge.

Earlier, I wrote 'for some people' the reading of a book is the way they will acquire knowledge. But equally, as a considerable amount of research has confirmed, some will never be able to learn from a book, even though they may be as literate as the others.

OPEN LEARNING

Books of a guiding nature are good for those who find this a satisfactory way of learning. The bookshops are full of them, covering a wide variety of subjects. Some offer too wide an approach for those individuals who require something tailored to their needs and it is here that the wide range of open learning systems may be more appropriate. This group includes:

- open learning packages, either distantly controlled or tutor-supported
- video programmes
- interactive video programmes
- computer programmes
- interactive computer programmes.

These systems can all be used at home or at work, provided the necessary hardware is available. There is no need to attend a training course and they offer exercises for the individual to enact. There are obvious differences between them, principally in the mode in which the exercise is offered rather than in the content.

A fairly typical programme of any of these systems would include input, in the particular mode, of the techniques and methods of, in this case, interviewing. This input would either precede or follow a scenario which includes the necessary learning points. In the written programmes this could take the form of a script between two people in an interactive situation; in the video an actual presentation of the situation; and on the computer again a verbal description possibly supported by graphics. The learner would then be asked to perform certain tasks; for example, in the text-based programme, to read the script and identify the structure, techniques and behaviours used and comment on their relevance. Or he might be required to consider a basic case and, from the information supplied, plan an interaction in the full range of required approaches. A similar system could be used with the computer program.

In the case of the video and perhaps the computer, the participant would watch the action and be required to comment or answer questions. Following interactive examples of these methods, after the participant had answered or taken other action, the video/computer would correct it or demonstrate the most appropriate action.

LEARNING ON THE JOB

In theory, the most effective method of learning is to use the actual work on which one is engaged as the learning instrument, and doing this at the workplace rather than on a training programme divorced from the work location. The principle of this approach is that the learner sits beside a skilled worker, Nellie/Fred, and watches the operation being performed until he feels sufficiently confident to have a try himself. In some situations it can help if Nellie/Fred also describes what is being done, how and why. When the time comes for the observer to try the operation, Nellie/ Fred will watch carefully and assess, with subsequent feedback, how well the job was done. This is the classical 'tell, show, do' situation.

Much of the success will depend on the skill of the job trainer (Nellie/Fred). They should be good operatives so that they can demonstrate efficient methods, but they should also have some training skills so that they can describe the operations clearly and accurately, and give realistic and helpful feedback. Unfortunately, the only criterion usually considered in the choice of the on-the-job trainer is 'Are they a good operator?'.

When all the criteria are fulfilled this approach works well with mechanical operations where there is one right way to do the job. But in human interactions each successful operator has their own personal 'right' way – a variation of style, words, attitudes etc. – in other words, there is not one 'right' way. For example, if you are watching someone perform a successful interview, the effective structure, techniques and general behaviours are exhibited and demonstrated. But the combination of these effects is very personal and may be difficult, if not impossible, to replicate.

THE TRAINING COURSE

It has become fashionable to decry the value of the training course as a learning process, by stating that it is a completely artificial environment, a poor atmosphere for learning and makes the transfer of learning difficult. There is no doubt that there are bad trainers and bad courses in existence with poor content and training methods. But there are also courses and trainers at the other end of the spectrum with excellent training and learning conditions within the unavoidable constraints. The principal advantage of the training course is that it brings together a group of people who can discuss mutual problems, learn as a group and cross-fertilize ideas and methods and, more than any other benefit, can practise their theoretical skills on each other.

The classical form of an interview training course is as follows:

1 Input sessions with or without discussion on the techniques, methods and behaviours as described in the first part of this book
2 Practice interviews using
   (*a*) artificial situations
   (*b*) real situations experienced by others
   (*c*) real situations experienced by one of the learners
   (*d*) real situations which are arising 'here and now'.

There are many variations on these themes. The knowledge input sessions can be straight lectures or highly participative events with the learners being actively involved in discussing and concluding themes initiated by the trainer. Or these can be replaced by the participants working out in small groups what they want in terms of structure etc.

Many courses, with a saving of time in mind, require pre-course learning in which the participants read material normally included in a full input session. On the course itself the knowledge areas consequently become summary or refresher sessions. Thus more time is made available for the real learning situations of the practice interviews.

There are different kinds of practice interviews with different objectives. In artificial situations the two participants act out roles which have been given to them by the trainers, roles which may or may not have any relation to their real life experiences. The role definition can vary from a simple description of a situation and the instruction 'Take it from there', to a detailed description of how to approach the interaction. The advantage of this role-play approach is that the case can be constructed in advance with the aim of ensuring that the relevant learning points emerge. The role players often perform more effectively in this situation since the threat level is reduced by the artificiality of the case. This can be a disadvantage as well as an advantage. As a disadvantage it gives the participants a means of self-defence if the interview goes badly. 'After all it wasn't real. I wouldn't have done that back at work in a real interview' or 'The information was too detailed and complex/not sufficiently detailed'.

A touch of reality can be brought to the course by selecting one of the participant's real cases. At the least this will negate any criticism that an artificial case study would never happen in real life. The 'owner' of the case can play either the interviewer or the interviewee, but the other person must be given full information about the situation so that they can behave realistically in the role. The role play can be enacted in the way in which it occurred, as it 'should' have occurred, or in an open, experimental way. On the disadvantage side, the role learning can be used as rationalization for failure and in a training-directed course, the case might not provide the desired learning points.

The midway approach is to use a real case but one which is not owned by either participant. This is similar to the constructed artificial case, but avoids the accusation of unreality. In all other aspects the advantages and disadvantages are similar to the constructed case.

The problem common to all three methods is that the participants have to *act* the role to a greater or lesser extent. The success of the interview may depend on acting ability, or how little regard is paid to the realization that it is an artificial situation. And, consequently, if the interview does not succeed, lack of acting experience or skill may be used as defence against criticism of the failure.

Feedback

The main advantage of learning the skills of interviewing on a training course is the opportunity not only to practise interactions in a group of people who are similarly motivated, but also to receive relevant and objective feedback. I have mentioned earlier the facility of using non-participants in the small group to observe and give the interviewer feedback on his performance. Incidentally this also gives the observers the opportunity to practise giving feedback, yet another skill which is utilized in many forms of interviewing. It is said by some that the observers learn as much, if not more, from the experience than the participants. I have reservations about this and it may be that with certain people or groups learning by observation may be limited.

One well-defined advantage which the practice interview has over the real interaction is that reaction feedback can be given immediately and directly by the person being interviewed. In real life it is rare that you will be told by the interviewee how well or badly you have done as an interviewer. Quite often you will be told, sometimes in no uncertain terms, how the other person has reacted to the things you have said, but not to your techniques, other than perhaps some reactions to your non-verbal communications.

After the practice interview there are numerous opportunities for feedback or appraisal of the interview techniques. On most training courses the interviewer is encouraged to assess his own performance and verbalize his thoughts for the benefit of himself and the others. When a learner is strongly encouraged to self-assess, it is often surprising to that learner and the listeners how much he has, mainly subconsciously, recorded about the performance. This self-assessment can be supplemented by the person who has had to 'suffer' the interviewer's new-found techniques and who can therefore report directly how they were received. Neutral observers can report on aspects which may not have been picked up by the interviewee/er. Finally, if there is anything remaining which has not already received comment and which deserves mention, or where learning points arise from the discussion, the tutor can enter with his contributions.

Non-human aids can also be introduced, either to supplement or replace the human comments. These may be audio cassette or video recordings which are capable of immediate and accurate recall of what was said and done. Used on their own the interviewer can, at his leisure, view his performance and assess his effectiveness objectively. Alternatively, the viewing can be in front of the group and the tutor when different and selected aspects of the interview can be discussed.

Whatever learning method is used, some form of feedback is invaluable because even the most apparently self-objective individual may have behavioural blind-spots, which can be illuminated by others who can see more clearly through the barriers. It may even be possible to obtain direct feedback in the real situation by asking the interviewee (or selected ones) if they could give any feedback on how they saw the process of the interview. In real life there is obviously considerable risk in giving this invitation, but the benefits can be well worthwhile. The question should be directed at the success of the process, not the interviewer's skill, as this might put the interviewee on the spot – what had been a semi-unreal situation would be forced to a very personal level. The interviewee may not be ready or prepared to move to this level.

BEING INTERVIEWED

An interview requires a minimum of two people – the interviewer and the interviewee. The emphasis in this book, in line with its objectives, has been on the role of the former, but consideration of the interviewee's role can help in two ways:

- the interviewee's likely reaction can be more accurately assessed
- most interviewers themselves may have been interviewees at times in their lives, so looking at interviews in which one has been involved can be part of the training process.

Those who have themselves been interviewers should be at some advantage when being interviewed. They should be aware of the different approaches to interviewing, have some ideas of the types of questions which might be asked, have an appreciation of the game-playing possible in an interview and, above all, be aware of the types of responses the interviewers are likely to be seeking.

Interviewees should prepare themselves for the

interview at least as thoroughly as the interviewer. They should be as flexible in the style and progress of their responses as the interviewer should be in leading the interview. They should be as capable as the interviewer at thinking quickly and behaving appropriately.

The principal consolation for an interviewee is that the interviewer is probably feeling equally nervous, uncomfortable and concerned about the interview. If the interviewer is not in this state then there is little the interviewee can do to affect the process of the interview – they can rely only on what they have to offer.

Consequently the role of the interviewee in, for example, a selection interview, is to

- ensure that his skills, attitudes and knowledge are presented in the most effective way.

If they are not, he has only himself to blame if he doesn't get the job (provided all other factors are equal). But to do so he must

- try to assess the aims, objectives, selection criteria of the interviewer by analysing the questions asked and the responses, verbal and non-verbal, to the answers given.

The interviewee should also try to assess what will happen during the interview, what questions will be asked, what answers should/will be given, what type of behaviour will be expected, what type of behaviour he wants to exhibit and so on.

THE SEVEN-POINT PLAN

A seven-point plan for interviewing has been commended in many training courses and, although not every interviewer follows this plan, most of the points come into most interviews in some way or other. The plan consequently provides a good basis for thinking about the interview before the event.

PHYSICAL ASPECTS

This section of the seven-point plan covers a variety of aspects some of which may affect the interviewee's attitude. Some will be obvious: jobs which require a lot of movement or extensive travel will demand a particular level of physique, appearance or health. The specific demands will leave little room for manoeuvre – if the job requires you to be 6 feet 3 inches tall and you are only 5 feet 10 inches, the result is foregone and obvious. But the interviewer will be looking for other items many of which will be assessed in the early stages of the interview. First impressions are known to be frequently inaccurate, but it is a well-researched and well-established fact that most of us are susceptible to forming first impressions which may be strong, impactive and which tend to stay.

Research suggests that many decisions are made in the first four minutes and the remainder of the interaction is taken up with attempts to substantiate these first impressions.

Unfortunately there is no way of assessing whether or not the interviewer is sensitive to the formation of significant first impressions, so you must assume that this is the case. Consequently you 'know' that as you enter the interviewing arena you are being observed and assessed on the basis of first impressions. Part of the preparation must then be your decision about how to enter, how to dress, what to do on entering, and the general impression you wish to give. How do you ensure this?

CIRCUMSTANCES

Some aspects of the job may not be evident from the public statement about the vacancy; for example, other requirements might relate to much more travelling than was indicated. In such a case you could expect to be asked whether there are any barriers which might not permit this amount of travelling and perhaps staying away from home overnight or longer. Similarly, if acceptance of the job requires removal to another area of the country, questions will certainly relate to any problems of relocation.

ATTAINMENTS

The part of the interview designed to obtain information about

- educational and professional qualifications
- post-employment experience, training and qualifications
- the history of the applicant's employment career, full-time, part-time or spare-time

is the start of the main questioning part of the interview. In this section the interviewer will use some or all of the techniques described to obtain the maximum amount of information from you, the interviewee.

The role of the interviewee is to give this information, but there must have been some consideration of

- how much information to give
- what information to give
- in what manner to give the information

The interviewee of course, is the holder of the information and it will be to his advantage to rehearse beforehand certain elements of which he should be aware:

- What type of information is the interviewer likely to seek? About school, college or university attainments? Can I remember all the important details?
- Questions will be asked about previous employment. Can I readily recall all the types of jobs I have done and what I thought about them? Which ones do I want to concentrate on? Are there any areas I want to avoid? How can I slip past them?
- If he asks closed questions, should I give closed answers? I shall have to be on the lookout for multiple questions and give information relating to all the parts.

Dates can be stumbling blocks for an interviewee,

particularly where a number of incidents are likely to be discussed; also the order in which the various activities occurred. Thought before the interview can clarify any unclear points in the interviewee's mind – not in the trauma of the interview itself.

SPECIAL APTITUDES AND INTERESTS

Movement by the interviewer into these areas will continue the basic pattern of the interview and again the interviewee must think beforehand about his achievements in special areas or perhaps work external to his normal occupation. Someone with a wide range of interests will be best advised to identify the principal ones, those which have greatest relevance to the work in question, or those which demonstrate a lively, different approach signifying adaptability. Sometimes, however, a complete listing of interests in a summary form may be necessary to indicate a breadth of capability and mental processes.

It is usually within this section of the interview that the really difficult or trick questions can emerge. They might penetrate areas of politics, religion, ethics, sexual and sexist attitudes, equal opportunities and many other areas of an individual's value beliefs and judgements. It is a difficult decision whether or not interviewers should open up this line of questioning. Often it may be because the interviewer does not know what else to ask; the interviewee may be having his sensitivity tested; or the interviewer may honestly want to assess their correlation with the attitudes and values existing in the organization.

The following list gives 129 awkward questions which interviewees have been asked in real interviews. How difficult would *you* find them to answer? Would you answer them? How would you answer them? The list can also serve, although perhaps it should not, as a guide to *interviewers* of some questions that they could ask.

The list is reproduced from the booklet *We'll Let You Know*, with the kind permission of the Manpower Services Commission and John Bowden, Charlotte Chambers and

Jane Marsh of the School of Management Studies, Polytechnic of Central London, who were commissioned to undertake the study by the MSC.

129 AWKWARD INTERVIEW QUESTIONS

1   We all miss opportunities. What have you missed?
2   What newspapers do you read?
3   What took your notice in today's papers?
4   How much television do you watch?
5   What are your strong points?
6   . . . and your weakest?
7   What books do you read?
8   Tell me about the last book you read.
9   To what do you attribute your present job hunting problems?
10 What did you learn from your last job?
11 Do you mind travelling?
12 Does you husband/wife mind you travelling?
13 If you had a better offer in two months' time, would you take it?
14 What happens if you get married?
15 . . . start a family?
16 . . . if your husband/wife moves would you go with him/her?
17 What do you look for when seeking a new job?
18 Bearing in mind the current difficult times, would you take a drop in salary?
19 Would you mind taking a psychological test?
20 Do you ever have any doubts as to your ability to do a job?
21 What appeals to you about this job?
22 What do you look for when interviewing your own staff?
23 Your handwriting seems to indicate that you are not a very stable person; what do you say to this?
24 I don't understand what makes you think you can do this job.
25 If salary and job satisfaction conflict, which would

you choose?
26   Are you a clubbable person or a loner?
27   Do you take work home? . . . daily? . . . weekends?
28   Do you have any money-making activities outside your job?
29   What action would you take if you disagree with a decision of a superior?
30   You seem to have 'stayed put' a long time. Is this now a handicap to you?
31   What was your last salary?
32   You seem to have moved around a lot. How do you account for it?
33   We cannot make a decision in less than five weeks and we will let you know then. Is that all right?
34   Would you describe your ideal boss?
35   Who was the nearest you had to it?
36   After a lifetime in one industry, do you regret moving out?
37   What would you consider a reasonable time to stay in a job?
38   What salary are you seeking?
39   Why did they select you for redundancy?
40   In your last job did you give yourself any personal objectives?
41   You must have been to other interviews – how does this one compare?
42   Do you intend to continue your education and studies?
43   When did you last buy a new suit?
44   Did you buy it on your own, or did your wife select it?
45   In your last company did they operate MBO?
46   Do you play any games?
47   How much is your pension?
48   Do you belong to any clubs?
49   Do you regard not having been to university a handicap?
50   Was your university training really worthwhile?
51   Does your wife work?
52   May we approach your employer for a reference?

53 Go back five years – what mistakes have you made?
54 You must have been for a number of jobs. Why have you not been successful?
55 When was the last time someone left your staff and why?
56 Do you find it a problem keeping up to date with technical advances?
57 Where do you expect to be in three years' time?
58 Do you have a health problem?
59 Why should we employ you in preference to other candidates?
60 May I be personal? You are overweight . . . flushed . . . not relaxed etc.
61 Were you happy in your last job?
62 How much influence has your wife/husband on your work?
63 Do you try to improve your work?
64 How?
65 Do you take part in politics?
66 How many friends do you have?
67 What annoys you?
68 What sort of boss do you know you could not work for? Who came nearest to it?
69 What are your realistic career aims?
70 Why do you prefer this particular job?
71 What is your strongest attribute in management terms?
72 . . . and your weakest?
73 As far as you are concerned personally, what do you think your major problem would be if you joined us?
74 Why did you apply for this job?
75 How do you get on with the opposite sex?
76 Would you prefer to be a small fish in a big pond or a big fish in a small pond?
77 What was the main weakness of your last boss?
78 How did it affect your work?
79 What did you do to compensate?
80 Why did you not achieve more in your last job?
81 What is your form of relaxation?

82 Have you any other offers you are considering at the moment?
83 What are the offers you are considering?
84 Why do you want this job?
85 Are you a good manager?
86 (To a man) Is your wife able to keep up with you intellectually, or is she mainly concerned with home?
87 Are you more of a craftsman, or an artist?
88 Do you think you could have done better in your last job?
89 Are you married? (answer 'no') Why not?
90 What are your greatest achievements?
91 When did you influence the profits of your employer most?
92 Would you tell us why you and your last employer parted? (after an explanation) Could you be more frank with us?
93 I am afraid you do not have the experience we are looking for.
94 What do you carry in your heavy briefcase?
95 If we were to offer you this position would you accept it?
96 To be frank with you, you are too old for this position.
97 Good morning, what can we do for you? What can you do for us?
98 Why did you leave your last employer?
99 I would like to consider you for this position, but I think you are too big for the job.
100 Do you tolerate fools easily?
101 Do you regard it as a weakness to blow your top?
102 What is the first thing you would do if you received an order for 350 thirty-five-gallon insulated hot water tanks?
103 You have a private income, don't you?
104 How important is a pension scheme to you?
105 Good morning, will you have a cup of coffee?
106 Good afternoon, Mr Jones (your name is Smith).
107 Good morning, have they looked after you?

108 Would you like to tell us about yourself?
109 Mr Archibald isn't available; I'm his assistant. He asked me to interview you.
110 Good morning, how much do you know about us?
111 Hullo, you had no trouble finding us?
112 May we use Christian names?
113 If you were able to have an ideal job, what would it be?
114 What is your social life like? Do you entertain?
115 Do you think you can do this job?
116 What are your views on management consultants?
117 To what extent do you drink?
118 How would you describe success?
119 Why do you want to work for us?
120 What do you know about our products?
121 You have not done this job before, have you?
122 What is your religion?
123 What do you see as your greatest personality defect?
124 If you joined us, how long could we rely on you to stay?
125 For what advice or assistance do your colleagues turn to you?
126 (Referring to confidential aspects of your present employer's products) What are your company's latest developments in the field of . . . ?
127 Why did you try for this job?
128 Have you ever been passed over for promotion?
129 No, surely you have not reached the top?

Attitudes to unemployment

One particularly common awkward question for many people concerns the reason for being unemployed.

How have people reacted to you being unemployed?

Where this has not been as you would have wished, what do you think the cause is?

- Embarrassment (yours or theirs)?
- Fear? If so, of what?
- Misunderstanding? What about?
- Feelings of inadequacy (yours or theirs)?
- Suspicion? If so, why?

INTELLIGENCE

The measure of an interviewee's intelligence can only be determined by psychological tests, not by their IQ. In some selection procedures applicants are required to undertake tests of intelligence, attitudes or aptitudes. But during the interview proper the measure of intelligence must be sought by examples of its practical application.

The types of question from which the interviewer will attempt to assess this quality will probably come into the list of awkward or difficult questions and may be expressed in the form of a hypothetical question. This should ideally be related to the interviewee's experience or to the work which he would be expected to perform. There are some interviewers who delight in the sight of the interviewee wriggling with embarrassment or unease.

Hypothetical questions may include the following:

If the budget of your work responsibility area was to be doubled (or halved), what would you do with the additional (reduced) finance?

One of your best workers has been found contravening an organization regulation for which heavy penalties are prescribed. What action would you take?

The initial hypothetical question may often be relatively simple, but the interviewer is likely to come back with a supplementary which usually gives further problems or raises barriers in the way of the initial reponse.

There is very little that the interviewee can do in advance to prepare for questions of this nature, except to guess that they may relate to certain obvious matters. Possible answers can then be formulated. But the interviewee must be aware during the event that if this type of question does arise, he will have to be careful with his answers and be prepared to be led along what the interviewer intends to be a road mined with behavioural traps. Although one must not become paranoid about situations of this nature, it is often the case that what appears to be a simple question can be, or can develop into, the most dangerous question in the interview.

DISPOSITION

This is the most difficult area for the interviewer to assess about you, the interviewee. He can only base any assessment on your behaviour during the interview, so you must ensure that you are signalling the image you intend to transmit – this is not always the case! Interviewees are often asked how well they 'get on with other people', or others with them. This is a rather ineffectual question if the interviewer hopes to receive completely honest information. Few people will answer that their relationships are poor, whether or not this is true, and whether or not the dishonest answer is given from an intention to deceive or a lack of self-awareness.

An interviewee will often give, subconsciously, signals which demonstrate, at least in that particular situation, the type of person he is. An interviewee can be verbose (when verbosity is not being sought); inarticulate (when the ability to describe, persuade or influence is being judged); hesitant, dogmatic, able to juggle concepts, able/unable to support expressed views, pleasant, irascible and so on. If the image presented is the one which

- the interviewer is seeking, and
- the interviewee is intending to project

all is well. But the two may be out of step and will result in the interviewee's rejection.

What can you do? It may sound simplistic and more difficult to perform than to say, but – modify your behaviour to suit the situation, or at least your assessment of the situation.

THE END OF THE INTERVIEW

At the end of the interview the interviewee may be asked if there is anything he wants to know which has not already been covered. He must then decide whether there is anything which he needs clarifying, and how he is going to pose the questions. Most of the potential questions in an interviewee's mind would probably have been answered naturally during the course of the interview. But if this has not happened and the interviewee does not raise them when given the opportunity, he is denying his own right to essential information. Some unscrupulous interviewers will deliberately omit an essential part of the interview and will wait to see if this is raised! On the whole, I think it is more acceptable to ask reasonable questions than to remain silent, even though all you can think of is how to get out of the interview room!

There are certain questions, however, which should not be asked. These are concerned with feedback on performance during the interview, e.g. 'How did I do?'; very personal questions or statements intended to impress: statements to give corrected information about subjects discussed earlier in the interview (unless they relate to a glaring error or omission), and questions about the immediate result of the interview.

A certain interview at which I was one of a small panel of interviewers ended with the invitation to ask questions. The interviewee asked 'Have I got the job?'. He knew that he was one of a number of people being interviewed and the convention was fully known to him that notification of success or failure would come later. He was not successful.

Whether you are to be the interviewer or the interviewee, the general principles are the same – prepare and plan in advance of the event. There is no guarantee that, however extensive, you will be able to cover every eventuality, but at least you will be prepared for some of the possibilities. Preparation will not always ensure success, but lack of it will almost certainly produce failure unless you are one of the minority of people with charisma. Interviews can be pleasurable or hellish, whichever side of the table you are seated. Skill, experience, practice will all go to ensure that there is more of the former than the latter. But do not avoid the experiences, rather seek out opportunities to practise. As in so many avenues of life, practice maketh perfect (or at least acceptable!)

Part II

Interviewing in Action

10 The counselling interview

Let us first consider the structure of the counselling interview. In most cases it will be initiated by the person with the problem rather than the manager. Consequently there will be little or no time for planning. However, the wise manager or supervisor will have developed an inbuilt strategy for structuring automatically any counselling event which might be forced upon them, which can then be applied immediately as the occasion arises.

As suggested earlier, the counselling of staff problems can take two basic forms – work related or personally based. Perhaps the most common *could* be the work-related problem, so the manager should be aware of his philosophy and structure for dealing with this type of problem.

WORK-RELATED PROBLEMS

The chain of events in the work-related problem usually starts with the worker approaching the manager or supervisor with a request for some time and help in solving a problem related to the work with which that individual is concerned. With the invitation to enter the room or other area the interview has started. No introductory period is necessary in this case as the reason for the problem solving is very clear, or at least appears to be so. Consequently the usual initial stage of this type of interview is one of *investigation* to determine the nature and extent of the problem. During this period, the interviewer will invite the interviewee to state the problem as he sees it. The investigation continues with attempts by the interviewer at complete clarification: this articulation of the problem has a two-fold benefit. Firstly, the interviewer is made aware of the extent of the problem and, secondly, gives the problem-owner the opportunity to clarify the details of the problem in his own mind by having to explain them to someone else. It is essential for this to take place because many problem-owners do not think through fully before shouting for help. Once the problem is completely expressed there is the possibility that no further help is necessary. The problem-owner, simply by describing it clearly, has come to a realization of the solution.

If, however, the solution is not readily available, the interview can move on to the next stage – that of *starting the problem-solving*. Here the interviewer has two options.

First because he has a higher level of skill and a greater experience than the problem-owner, the dialogue could continue as follows:

> Interviewer: 'Right, that's the problem. What now?'
> Interviewee: 'Well boss, what do you think I should do about it?'
> Interviewer: 'This is what you do. First you . . . Then you . . . and finally you . . . '
> Interviewee: 'That's great, boss. Thanks a lot.'

(*a*) The interviewee exits feeling delighted that the problem is solved.

However, there are other possible feelings on the part of the interviewee on being told what to do:

(*b*) the interviewee exits saying to himself 'That was a lot of use; I knew all that before I went in' or

(*c*) interviewee exits saying to himself 'That might be what he wants, but I'm going to do it this way'.

In the alternatives (*b*) and (*c*), the interview has obviously been a waste of time. Although it is not so immediately obvious, alternative (*a*) has been equally a waste of time if the longer term is considered. Certainly the problem has been solved successfully and the interviewee is

satisfied, but there is the danger that the manager has lost an excellent opportunity to coach and develop the worker.
Consider the second option:

> Interviewer: 'Right, that's the problem. What now?'
> Interviewee: 'Well boss, what do you think I should do?'
> Interviewer: 'You must have given some thought to the possible solutions. Have you any ideas yourself?'
> Interviewee: 'I'm not sure boss, but one thing we might be able to do is . . . '.

In this way the problem has been put back to where it belongs, with the problem-owner, and the interviewee's problem-solving capabilities have been developed by ensuring that the worker rather than the boss works through from the problem to the solution.

Even this may not be the best progression of the interview, as most problems usually have more than one possible solution and the one offered may not be the best one. So the second stage is more correctly *the generation of alternative solutions*. With this structure the dialogue would continue:

> Interviewer: 'OK, that's one solution. Is that the only one or are there any other possible approaches?
> Interviewee: 'Well, er, I did think that perhaps . . .'.
> Interviewer: 'Great. Any others?'
> Interviewee: 'No. I can't think of any more.'
> Interviewer: 'We could always have a look at . . .'.

The interview has now opened up the whole approach to the problem and several possible solutions have been generated. It would now be simple for the interviewer to select one of the solutions and prescribe that this should be put into operation. But this could have the same effect as the prescription at the earlier stage. Instead, a further stage of the counselling approach can be entered, which can be described as *solution selection*. During this stage the two interactors can discuss the advantages and disadvantages of each possible solution. At the end of the stage, the discussion could be in the form of:

> Interviewer: 'So we have discussed all the possible solutions. Which one do you see as the most effective?'
>
> Interviewee: 'From my practical experience of the work, I suggest that . . .'.

If the interviewer also feels that this would be the best solution, the discussion can then continue. If however, the boss felt that this suggestion was not right for the situation, the comparisons could be resumed.

The next stage, after the selection has been made, concerns the final decision, the action description and the summary – the *conclusion*.

When problems are brought to the boss for solution, they are not always so complex that a number of possible solutions need be considered. But the counselling approach can and should still be used even in these circumstances, otherwise the developmental opportunity is lost.

The interview in this case would start as before with a statement of the problem and any clarification which might be necessary. The solution generation could then be sought, but where the interviewee is not very experienced the more experienced boss might have to take the lead. For example:

> Interviewer: 'We now know the full extent of this problem. What ideas have you?
>
> Interviewee: 'I've looked and looked at this and I just can't see a way out.'
>
> Interviewer: 'Can you think of anywhere you might go to in order to get a lead?'
>
> Interviewee: 'Not really.'
>
> Interviewer: 'What do you think about the idea of looking in the precedents file?
>
> Interviewee: 'Yes, I could do that and also . . . Thanks boss.'

In this case, although some guidance has been given by the boss, the greater part of the work and some consideration of other aspects have fallen squarely on the shoulders of the problem-owner. Even when the boss put forward the idea, it was suggested in a format so that the interviewee had to respond rather than agree or disagree. This is the principal emphasis of most effective counselling interviews – put the problem analysis and solution provision back to the problem-owner as much as possible and keep on putting it back until nothing more can be achieved by this process.

The benefits of this form of counselling can be for both the boss and the worker. The workers are encouraged to solve the problems themselves and consequently grow and develop in their skill and knowledge. The principal benefits to the boss are that he is not always forced to produce decisions or solutions, he has opportunities to develop his staff and eventually he will reduce the number of demands on his time. If his staff develops to the extent that they become sufficiently skilled to solve problems themselves or know when they need to look elsewhere for the answers, there will be reduced interference for the boss.

In summary the stages for resolving work-related problems are as follows:

Introduction
Statement of the problem
Clarification of the problem
Generation of possible solutions
Discussion of alternative solutions
Decision on acceptable or most effective solution
Action agreed
Summary.

PERSONAL COUNSELLING

Not all problems brought for counselling are solely work related. Many, depending on the relationship which the boss might have with his subordinates, will relate to personal problems, although these might often have a knock-on effect with the work. The way in which the boss approaches these requests for counselling of the more

personal matters will depend on his philosophy of interest
and involvement in the well-being of his staff.

The personal counselling interview follows very closely
the one on work-related matters, except that the statement
and clarification of the problem may need to be more
extensive and intensive.

People who need personal counselling are often in a
highly emotional state. Consequently an introductory
period may be beneficial in which the main objective is to
settle the interviewee down so that he is in a state of mind to
talk lucidly. This may appear contradictory – why else
would the individual request an interview for the very
purpose of talking about the problem? Two factors may be
relevant here: their emotional state as a result of the
problem may be so confused that they may not be able to
articulate their thoughts in a rational manner. Or, again an
apparent contradiction, even though an interviewee has
sought to talk over a problem, it is often the last thing he
wants to do. This latter factor can overcome the openness
of the individual so that some problem is exposed,
counselled and solved, usually a relatively simple, work-
related problem. However, once this has happened and the
individual is on the way out, often with a hand on the door
handle he turns and says 'Oh, by the way, there was
something else if you have a moment'. When this happens
the counsellor should be aware that the real problem is
about to emerge. It is therefore a wise move to invite the
individual to sit down (again), for if indeed this is the case,
a substantial counselling session is ahead.

The personal problems brought to the caring manager
can range widely from relationship problems within the
office of works, through financial, travelling and social
problems, to the delicate domestic or marital problems. In
many cases, the only possible interim solution is to
recommend reference to a specialist welfare organization
or such source of help as the local authority social services.
Many large companies have their own internal welfare
officers and if the manager feels that he is getting out of his
depth, an adjournment of the meeting might be agreed so
that this specialist can be introduced. But some people will

always prefer that the manager whom they know deals with them, rather than a stranger, however much a specialist they might be. Managers should therefore be aware of the range of external services available with expert help.

In this area of counselling more than any the interviewer will encounter strong emotional attitudes and feelings during the interview as the problem unfolds and the reality of the problem overcomes its owner. When the interviewee is under stress this will often take the form of tears, in either men or women Many managers admit that when somebody breaks down and cries in front of them, they are completely at a loss and often do something which does not seem to help. The psychological reason for tears is that they are a mechanism for releasing the tension, pressure and stress building up in the individual. It is therefore best to allow this cathartic release, in fact it is possible that some damage may result if it is inhibited. Practical experience certainly bears this out. I have talked with many men and women who admit to having broken down in this way during an interview and, without exception, they said that what they wanted and needed when this occurred was to be left alone to get on with it and cry their emotion out. Similarly many managers who have been the recipient of the tears say that their most successful ploy was to let the crying run its course and act thereafter as if it were a completely natural event (which it is). Acknowledge that the occurrence has not disturbed the interviewer, other than help him to realize the depth of the emotion within the interviewee.

Some counselling interviews are initiated by the manager rather than the problem-owner. Examples of these are approaches to a member of the staff who is not progressing as well as he should be, but not for any reason which would require disciplinary action. A typical case might be a recent promotion to a level which requires a complete attitudinal change on the part of the promotee and a variation of working methods. The individual may not make these changes without a counselling interview from which a plan of action could result. An observant manager or supervisor might notice that a worker is behaving differently from normal and suggest that he might be having problems or is under some form of stress. Problems which are becoming, unfortunately, all too common at work are those of alcoholism and drug addiction.

In these problems the manager or supervisor has to initiate some action or series of actions, the first of which is usually a direct counselling interview. Two choices are presented to the manager, depending on whether the basic problems develop into work-related ones. Personal troubles must remain private to the individual unless he is willing to be counselled or the problem is adversely affecting the work.

If none of the above problems is affecting the work in any way, the manager might feel that he has no responsibility in broaching the subject. A caring approach can often be regarded as an intrusion of privacy. However, some will argue that to ignore a problem is to ignore a responsibility for ensuring that a problem which *at that time* does not affect the work, does not do so in the future. Early action may avoid subsequent trouble at a stage when it is too late to produce effective action. This may often be the case where an individual has a personal problem involving, for example, finance, marriage, parents etc. The problem-owner may have no one or know of no organization to which to turn. The counsellor can at least point that person in the right direction without becoming directly involved.

The situation is obviously more clear cut if the problem is directly affecting the work or work relationships. A normally polite and pleasant worker with customer contact is known to have a personal problem which is making him edgy and sharper than usual when dealing with people. This might develop to the stage where his approach to the customer becomes unacceptable and the first steps of discipline must be taken. If the individual's manager or supervisor had been aware of the development, a counselling interview would perhaps have prevented more drastic steps.

The interventionist role of the manager or supervisor becomes less clear when dealing with the alcoholic, although the same criteria must apply in that an individual has the right to damage himself through alcohol or drug abuse. It is only when the effects of the abuse exhibit themselves at work and affect either the work or fellow-workers that the senior person has the absolute right to take action. Counselling, rather than discipline must be the first approach.

In manager-initiated interviews there is obviously more opportunity for planning – gathering the known facts, ensuring that all effects have been substantiated, deciding on a method of approach and having or obtaining knowledge of some of the problem-solving agencies. The interview can even be arranged in many cases for the most propitious time for both parties.

Knowledge that a person for whom you have responsibility has a serious and developing problem, can often come as the result of a comment or report by a third party, perhaps a colleague. The information may be passed on to you, not for any trouble-making reasons, but as the result of a caring and helping concern. In these cases it is useful to seek as much third-party information as possible, always bearing in mind that some of it might be suspect. The information may initiate some preliminary investigation into the scope and availability of helping agencies.

BEHAVIOUR

We have looked at the planning for the counselling interview technique in terms of structure. What can we do in planning the behaviour which might be exhibited? The objectives for this type of interview must be:

> To encourage the interviewee to express the problem as widely and as openly as possible
> To discuss and agree possible solutions with the interviewee (the solutions to come, preferably, from the interviewee).

We are looking for the following behaviour from the person who has requested the interview:

- Giving information, about the problem and everything connected with it
- Proposing alternative solutions
- Stating feelings and views about the solutions
- Proposing a final solution.

In order to produce this desired behaviour we must:

- Seek information: ask for a description of the problem
- Probe: obtain a complete definition of the problem
- Reflect: encourage the interviewee to talk
- Seek ideas: how might the problem be solved
- Support/build/disagree with reasons: reaction to the proposals made
- Seek proposals for the finally agreed solution
- Summarize the agreed actions.

But above all be prepared to listen very carefully and thoroughly.

We are less likely to achieve our objectives if we use the following categories of behaviour:

Blocking – facetious comments will be completely out of place

Attacking – the response to this is likely to be withdrawal into silence on the part of the interviewee

Disagreeing – if without reasons, the problem owner is likely to reject the counsellor and the counselling

Proposing – if the problem owner cannot produce ideas, the counsellor might wish to do so. Proposals in the form of prescribed statements may be rejected or even if apparently accepted will, through lack of commitment, be eventually ignored. If the counsellor has to produce some ideas, the more appropriate approach would be to put them in the form of questioning suggestions: 'How do you feel about the idea of doing . . .?'. This approach puts the onus of decision back where it belongs, with the problem owner, rather than putting the counsellor into the high risk position of prescribing solutions, or appearing to do so.

MODIFICATION OF THE PLAN

Of course, the interview may not go according to this plan – the interviewee might be very reticent or may have no ideas to put forward. As suggested earlier, if the circumstances are different from those which were planned, it is easier to modify the plan rather than have to suddenly think what to do in the trauma of an unexpected reaction. Let us say that we have reached the stage in the interview when we are encouraging the interviewee to offer possible solutions. Whichever approach is used and whatever pressure is applied, the interviewee will not or cannot suggest anything. If this inability is real, the interviewer is forced to offer his own solutions. Even then the continuance of the plan can still be attempted by suggesting rather than prescribing. The interviewee may still not react, so the final approach of prescribing has to be taken. Even then the plan is not lost. The proposal and its subsequent support by the interviewee signify one stage only. Once the proposal action is complete, the original approach can be attempted again, first with a seeking of ideas and, if this fails, further suggesting. The benefit of the plan is that it reminds the interviewer what he should be doing.

INTERVIEW LEVELS

The counselling interview is usually a sensitive event and early approaches by the counsellor must be cautious until it is obvious that the interviewee wishes to expose his feelings. Thus although a counselling interview by its very nature requires exposure at the deepest levels, this descent must be made gradually and with extreme care. Each level must be approached gently and any further movement delayed until it is certain that progress to the next level is acceptable to the interviewee. Always remember that although a counsellor might be approached by the other person for help, the problem owner often has great difficulty in opening the subject to scrutiny and will avoid talking about the problem for as long as possible. This avoidance of exposing the problem, even though the owner desperately wants it to be solved, can reach the extreme where the real problem does not emerge.

In this case it may emerge through the door-handle approach described earlier or, if there is no emergence on that occasion, a further approach might be made. The counsellor must be on the lookout for situations such as this, otherwise he is not fulfilling the role which the problem-owner has imposed upon him – that of a person who will surely help.

11 Selection, promotion and exit interviews

The aim of a selection interview is usually to choose from a number of applicants for employment the one most suitable for the post. The selection process may be for a post from within or without the organization. Alternatively the interview may be conducted by an external employment agent, for example, Professional and Executive Recruitment of the Manpower Services Commission. Whichever the situation, the approaches are very much the same. Derivatives of the basic recruitment interview are 'promotion' interviews within an organization, either to affirm suitability of the applicants for promotion or to select an applicant for promotion to a specific post.

APPLICATION FORMS

In cases of straightforward recruitment of external (and in most cases internal) applicants for employment, the applicants are required to complete before the interview, an application form with basic information such as name and address, age, marital status, educational history including academic qualifications and career history. Some application forms require the bare minimum of in-formation, others demand considerable detail of at least the educational and career histories. It is usually, although not always, the case that the interviewer will wish to extend this information through questioning. In the case of the longer and more detailed form, the interviewer will confirm the major details and select specific items to discuss further before moving on to aspects not covered in the form. Receipt of the application form well in advance of the interview will allow it to be used in the planning stages of the interview process.

Most application forms are of a fairly standard content, although some extend the basic details by asking about interests external to the work area and may ask for mini-essays on selected subjects. The principal criteria to remember are

- ask for information which relates to the employment
- the more detail requested the more information to digest on the return of the form.

As far as the first criterion is concerned, non-essential information represents a significant waste of time for both the interviewer and the interviewee, and the interviewee may be disturbed about the reason for such information being sought. Questions of this nature are often included by interviewers who wish to appear superior: unfortunately for them, they usually do more harm than good.

The application form has two uses:

- a preliminary sorting device to exclude from the time-consuming interview process those applicants who obviously do not satisfy the prime conditions
- an interview subject selector.

INITIAL STEPS – JOB SPECIFICATION

Before the application form question is raised, the reason for the selection interview must be determined. This will be triggered by either an existing employee leaving or an increase of work necessitating the engagement of additional employees. Immediate questions arise which must be answered before progress can be made:

- Do we really need a replacement?
- Can the work be shared out among remaining employees?
- Does the work still need to be done?
- Do we need new employees?
- Would it be more effective to retrain existing employees to the new work (and replace if necessary the existing employees)?

If consideration of these questions produces a positive answer, the next stage will be to identify those aspects of the work for which the new employee is required. The basic source of this information is the job description, supplemented as necessary by the post description. From this comprehensive information about the knowledge, skills and attitudes necessary to perform the job effectively, an interview job specification can be prepared.

If the information is not available or is incomplete, or perhaps no one has ever thought about producing such an analysis, the first stage will be to produce analyses of the task, the job and the post. Much will depend on the nature of the job as to the types of analyses required and how they are obtained. Job and task analyses are extremely important, wide-ranging and sometimes difficult to produce. There are a number of practical guides to assist would-be analysts and the subject is covered in Chapters 2 to 5 of one of my other books (*How to Measure Training Effectiveness*, Leslie Rae, Gower 1986). Further references are given there and in the bibliography to this book.

The job specification extracts from the various analyses a profile of the main features of the job which can be used to match the desired profile of the person who will fill the vacancy. Attention must be paid in drawing up the person profile to any relevant legislation – equal opportunities for men and women, racial discrimination, disabled persons, Factories Acts, Wages Councils, women and young persons etc., plus any relevant trade unions agreements.

INITIAL ACTION – PERSON PROFILE

The job specification, narrowed to define the main aspects of the job, forms one part of the necessary planning information. Now we need to know the nature of the person whom we shall want to fill this vacancy. The production of this profile used to be described, before sex discrimination, as a 'man specification' as opposed to the task orientation of the 'job specification' or 'work specification'. The term in common use at the present time is 'profile', hence 'person profile'.

If the interview is to produce the most acceptable result, the person profile must be realistically defined. During periods of high unemployment many highly qualified people are unable to find employment commensurate with their qualifications. It is a great temptation to employ people with the highest qualifications, even though that level of ability is not required in the job. This can be a dangerous practice. If the employment level eventually increases the over-qualified people might leave to obtain commensurate work, or because they have become bored or frustrated with a low demand job. On the other hand, the employment position may not improve significantly and employees may have to satisfy themselves with work which is less demanding than that which they would normally undertake.

With realism in mind, an effective approach to person profiling is to use the seven-point plan referred to in Chapter 8.

Physical requirements

Are there any particular requirements of physique, health, strength etc. without which the job could not be fulfilled? This criterion must be strictly enforced in order to avoid over-selection. It may also be necessary to ask 'If the most suitable applicant in every other way does not satisfy the physical requirements of the job, can the job be modified in any way?' I can recall a wheelchair-bound person with a disability of the legs who was suitable in every way for a particular light engineering job with a small company. The problem was that he was unable to reach and work at the bench alongside the other workers. The employer was persuaded with little difficulty to construct a lower section of the bench, fully fitted, at a comfortable height and width for the disabled person. There are many examples of modifications of this nature when the need and the will arise, but of course they are not always possible. For example, where a major aspect of the work depends on the identification of colour codes and the codes cannot be expressed in any other way, applicants with colour deficiencies cannot adapt to the work.

Educational attainments

Does the job require a particular level of education in order to be performed satisfactorily? Are professional qualifications required? Are both of these requirements real or perhaps traditional? It is certainly in this area of consideration that over-qualified recruitment is likely to occur as described earlier, although on occasions it is unavoidable. The question must always be: 'What is the lowest qualification I need? Do I necessarily require an applicant for this job, which has no possible promotion opportunities, to have that level of qualifications?

Work attainments

In the same way we must question the need for work-related attainments, although these are usually more specifically defined. Must the applicant have served an apprenticeship? Do the regulations for the work demand the possession of technical or professional recognition?

Experience

What the applicant has done previously, how effectively, to what level and so on must be the most important points to determine. A realistic job specification will show clearly the applicant's required experience. It will itemize the relevant knowledge and skills which will be determined in an effective interview and will show whether the two profiles match.

Special abilities

In addition to the routine nature of the work, and every job has these aspects, there may be some special abilities that the applicant has done or can demonstrate. Artistic ability is normally considered to be a special aptitude and if this is part of the job requirement, the applicant may be asked to produce a personal portfolio of his work.

Intelligence

The job may require a degree of what is commonly described as intelligence, over and above the normal requirements. Psychological tests may demonstrate the innate level of this intelligence, or the interviewee's responses to relevant testing questions may suggest this ability. In many cases this aspect must be taken on trust or assumption until it can be tested in the real situation: the value of intelligence is not in its possession, but in its application.

Disposition

It is important to decide whether a particular job requires a person who can exhibit a certain type or style of behaviour, manner or attitude. For example, salesmen, PR personnel, trainers or teachers, in addition to other qualifications, require certain social abilities. Disposition is as difficult to assess as intelligence. Most jobs which demand a particular form of behaviour in their performance are well-known. It is therefore reasonable to suppose that the applicant would exhibit the overt aspects of that behaviour, for at least the period of the interview. Again this performance must be taken on trust in the absence of any contrary evidence.

It is unfortunate that our ability to get to the root of a person's behaviour in a relatively short period of time is so limited, in view of its importance. Many jobs require a high degree of knowledge and skill which the job-holder may possess. But his standard will be below the effective or required level, or may even fail, if he cannot relate to, persuade or influence other people necessary to the performance of the job.

Circumstances

Job circumstances may often be related to time. Can the applicant work long or unsocial hours? Are there any obstacles to prevent the applicant from going to the other end of the country or perhaps flying abroad at short notice? Can he travel to work easily during normal and abnormal hours? Questions such as these should create little problem in the asking and the answering, but this is an area where the interviewer can fall foul of restrictive legislation. It would be unwise, for example, for an interviewer to ask a woman if she was married if (*a*) this had nothing to do with the employment, and (*b*) men were not asked the same question, for the same reason.

Consequently once the job requirements are specified, a person profile to match the job can be produced. The interview should result in an apparent profile of the applicant. If the two profiles match, or closely relate, here is a possible successful applicant for the job. *If* every job specification was exact; *if* every applicant was completely open; *if* . . . But rarely do these aspects coincide, so a further factor of the interviewer's subjective judgement must be introduced – and how wrong we can be at times!

Planning

We have already considered three aspects of the planning process – the application form, the job specification and the person profile. Apart from the physical arrangements for the interview, the remainder of the planning process is concentrated on the structure of the process, the behaviour necessary to obtain the required results and the level of approach.

Structure

The objectives of a selection interview are twofold:

- to determine whether the applicant is suitable for the job and the organization
- to determine whether the job and the organization are right for the applicant.

In order to achieve a decision on those objectives, the interview must be penetrating and closely linked to the reactions of the interviewee. Therefore, the process of the interview must be flexible, at the same time following the recommended basic structure of:

- Introduction
- Job information giving
- Applicant information seeking
- Winding up
- Termination

Introduction. Every interview has an opening and with a few exceptions it is usual to settle the applicant down so that the best can be made of the occasion. It is psychologically important in an interview to encourage the applicant to talk as much and as early as possible. Thus it is necessary to break the ice in some relevant manner. The approach will relate to the person being interviewed – some people resent starter questions, others welcome them, so whichever is used the interviewer must be on the lookout for reaction signals. Remember also that you too may need a settling down period. Typical 'safe' starter questions may be concerned with checking the person's name, any difficulties they had in finding the interview location, whether there are any objections to notes being taken and so on. And of course do not forget to introduce yourself. This omission has occurred on occasions and certainly on one when the interviewee knew in advance the name of the interviewer, but the interviewer was changed at the last minute!

On the subject of notetaking, which worries some interviewers, my advice is not to be too concerned over it. It has been suggested that interviewees can be disturbed by the interviewer taking notes – no doubt some can be, but my experience is that almost all are not concerned, in fact they may be expecting it. But there are some caveats.

Firstly, as suggested earlier, the practice of notetaking must be cleared with the interviewee at an early stage. Notetaking, once the interview is under way, must be brief and unobtrusive – even an interviewee who has readily agreed to the taking of notes will start to be concerned if it appears that his words are being recorded verbatim. Also, the more the interviewer is concentrating on the notes, and these will always lag behind the spoken word, the less he may be listening. Take notes of factual information only, not feelings or descriptions of personal or sensitive events. If it is necessary to record these, remember them and do so after the interview. Finally, if the interviewee says something which is detrimental to himself, do not record it immediately but wait until something else is said which the interviewee would probably want to be recorded, then record the earlier information.

There is no golden rule concerning the duration of this introductory part of the interview; it should last for as long as the need exists. There will probably be clues as to when the interviewee has started to relax. Most interviewees (and interviewers!) are nervous at the start of an interview, a state which may be broadcast by the non-verbal signals of fidgeting with the feet, hands or seating, a nervous 'look', and gestures such as smoothing an item of dress or the hair.

Verbal nervousness may exhibit itself by a catch in the voice, throat hoarseness or even difficulty in getting the words out. However, these signs may not always be related to nervousness, although they are common symptoms. The interviewer must watch to determine whether they are exhibitions of temporary or long-term behaviour. When signs of nervousness are reduced in intensity it is time to move on to the next stage.

Job information giving. An advertisement of a vacancy may give only brief details of its nature and any job can vary considerably in its practice between organizations, or even between departments. Whether or not a full job description has been given beforehand, either in the advertisement or in a brief issued to applicants before the interview, it is useful to describe the job in reasonable detail at the start of the interview. The time spent on this description serves several purposes: it allows the interviewer to settle down while giving factual information; it also gives the interviewee time to settle and ask questions; and, not least, the chance to realize that the job might not really be for him and to terminate the interview before too much time has been wasted.

One of the dangers for the interviewer is that he may dominate the interview at this stage by talking too much. It is preferable to say too little about the job and give the interviewee the opportunity to fill in any blanks with questions.

Information seeking. This will probably be the most substantial part of the interview and it will certainly be the most important. During this stage the interviewer will be obtaining information, views, feelings, opinions, attitudes etc. from the interviewee. And the interviewee will be trying to make the best possible impression. The former will be using the interviewee's responses to make an assessment and to produce a person profile to match with that of the job specification.

The content of the information seeking will depend on a variety of factors: the nature of the job, the qualifications required, the experience of the applicants and their qualifications, the interviewer's approach and the response profile of the applicant; the time allotted to the interview and so on. A logical but flexible plan of action is advisable – I have always found the seven-point plan or minor variations of it perfectly suitable for this purpose. Whatever the approach it should match the method used in obtaining the person profile for the job so that an easy comparison is possible.

Winding-up. This stage as far as the interviewer's role is concerned can be mercifully short, but time must be allowed for the interviewee to assume a dominant role.

Much of the interviewer's action at this stage is internal: he will be summarizing what information has been obtained and whether it is sufficient to make a decision. If not, any omissions can then be rectified. If the interviewer is satisfied that he is in possession of all the necessary information, the structure formula, by tradition, requires that the interviewee is asked if there is anything further he wishes to know or to say. Once any points have been cleared, the interview can move to the final stage.

Termination. It is often said that an effective approach to any communication is to KISS – an acronym for Keep It Short and Simple. This principle can certainly be adopted in the termination of an interview. Once it becomes obvious that all communication, either way, has been completed, the interview must be terminated firmly and the interviewee allowed to leave.

If the method of notification of the result of the interview has not already been detailed, the interviewee should be told what to expect next; when and how he will be notified; and how expenses will be cleared (if not already done so outside the interview).

The interviewee should then be thanked for attending and shown out of the room.

Some interviewers find it difficult to wind up and this problem usually exhibits itself by the interviewer starting to ask questions again or go over ground already covered.

Lack of skill or experience often produces a lack of self-confidence on the part of the interviewer. He may be unsure whether he has obtained all the information required. A confident interviewer ensures that all that he requires is obtained at the relevant stage and does not have to start going round in circles.

Post-interview action. Once the interviewee has left the room and before the next one enters (if there are several to be seen), some assessment must be made – at the very least a rough matching in quantifiable terms of the applicant against the job. Ratings can be given either for the full issue or against the different needs of the job. These ratings can be as scientific as the interviewer wishes; they are only an internal guidance system on which to make his decision.

One method is to allocate a total score to each applicant: e.g. 100, 150, 125, 175. The one with 175 marks will be offered the job and, because the marks are from a possible score of 200, very little further action will be necessary. If the second ranker with 150 has to be offered the job, the differential suggests that further training may be necessary.

Points or other ratings, with some system of weighting, can be allocated for identifiable parts of the job. For example, a salesperson's profile might include

Presence (including appearance)	95×2	$= 190$
General manner	90×3	$= 270$
Product knowledge	50	$= 50$
Influencing skills	80×2.5	$= 200$
Sales techniques	60×1.5	$= 90$

The scores as shown have a weighting which is shown as the $\times$ factor according to the requirements of the job or post. For example, product knowledge may or may not be of prime importance – in the example shown it has little because there is an extensive training programme to satisfy this requirement. Personal presence may have great or little value – all sales may be performed over the phone. And so on until a total score is obtained for each applicant.

BEHAVIOURAL PLANNING

In most selection interviews the behaviours which the interviewer can plan will be relatively straightforward, as should be the responses from the applicant. The plan for the interviewer which will normally require very little modification will include:

Seeking information – at the start of the interview
Giving information – about the job etc.
Seeking information – encouraging clarification questions from the applicant about the information given
Testing understanding – checking that the applicant has all the necessary information
Seeking information, views, feelings, opinions etc. – the main part of the interview
Reflecting – to encourage the applicant to talk, if necessary
Testing understanding – checking that the interviewee's understanding is complete
(Internal summarizing) – has all the information been obtained
Seeking information – (*a*) obtaining omitted information; (*b*) encouraging questions for information from the applicant
Giving information – final details of what will happen next.

The behavioural pattern of the applicant is anticipated to be straightforward responses to the interviewer's behaviour:

Giving information – in response to the initial settling-down questions
Seeking clarification/Testing understanding – asking questions about aspects of the job which may not have been clarified
Giving information – in response to questions, reflections and testing understanding from the interviewer in the main body of the interview

Seeking information – asking any final questions about aspects which have not been covered sufficiently

DISCUSSION LEVEL

The level which the interview will attain or at which it is aimed will depend on the nature of the job involved. Issues will need to be probed to a deeper level if the job is one of, say, personal adviser to the managing director, rather than a straighforward technical one of a capstan operator. In the case of the latter the discussion will be concerned mainly with factual information at levels 1 and 2, with occasional excursions as necessary into level 3. In the former case, most of the real discussion will be at levels 4 and 5 since it will be necessary for attitudes and motivations to emerge.

PROMOTION PANEL INTERVIEWS

Many organizations use promotion panels in order to select internally employed people for vacant posts. Most industrial and commercial organizations use this procedure to fill vacancies with applicants who are recommended or may have been invited to apply.

In government organizations such as the Civil Service recommended candidates are interviewed by a promotion panel in order to produce a list from which individuals are promoted during the currency of the list. In this method there is usually the additional facility for appeal against non-invitation for interview (and also non-selection, having been interviewed) particularly where the applicant is otherwise qualified.

The interviewee usually finds himself face to face with a number of interviewers – three is a favourite number for the panel – who ask questions for a period ranging upwards of twenty minutes.

Panel interviewers have the advantage over normal selection interviewers in that they are able to study the personnel records and recommendations for the applicant. In essence the interview is intended to confirm the written reports and to test the candidate under live conditions. Questions over a wide range of subjects, including the interviewee's past and present duties, determine how the interviewee can cope with these questions, to what level of understanding or creativity he can take them, and how he will cope with probes into his initial responses, perhaps with some degree of pressure. If a candidate goes to pieces under the pressure of the interview itself, the argument is that he could do the same in work pressure situations.

The structure and behaviour plans for a panel interview are similar to those for a selection interview. The objectives are equally similar: to select the most suitable candidate(s) for the posts or the lists. Usually the settling-down process is conducted by the chairman of the panel who asks the candidate non-threatening questions such as those about his current job. The main information-seeking questions come from the supporting members. The chairman is again involved towards the end of the interview with questions of his own, clarification questions about earlier matter or testing questions when it is difficult to assess the candidate on what has occurred to that stage. At the end of the interview the chairman will ask the candidate whether he has any questions or wishes to say anything more.

Assessment, whether for specific posts or for waiting lists, is usually based on a rating against a pre-determined level. Let us say that the level agreed in relation to the required numbers to be appointed or listed is 300. Those candidates who do not achieve this score will not be eligible to appear on the success list or waiting list; those with a score of 300 or more will therefore appear on the lists; those with the highest scores, say 400 to 500, will have demonstrated the highest ability, flexibility or acceptability. The base score of 300 is not, of course, a sacrosanct figure. If the candidates are of such high quality that too many achieve 300+ scores, the base level may have to be increased to 350 or more to contain the necessary successes. The level of the base score is usually determined by the prevailing economic or other demand requirements.

EXIT INTERVIEWS

Some managers have doubts as to the wisdom of holding what are known as exit interviews, that is to say with people who have given notice to leave their employment. The argument is that if someone is leaving the employment then that is their concern and attempts to discuss the situation are not only a waste of the employer's time but may also cause embarrassment.

The stage beyond taking no notice of the reasons for leaving is to ask the employee to complete a termination form stating these reasons. If the form is completed, usually there is no compulsion, it may be stored and used simply as statistical analysis for the board. This is a superficial approach at best and is really not more than a token attempt at information gathering. It avoids taking a more personal step with the leaver. Of course, there is no guarantee that the information given by the leaver is accurate and not facetious, if not actually and deliberately misleading.

The obvious action is to interview the leaver to determine the real reason for the termination of employment. This could be a traumatic experience for either the interviewer or interviewee, or both, and care has to be taken in deciding who should be the interviewer. Much will depend on the circumstances of the leaving and, in the first instance, the apparent reason. If there is no known rancour or bitterness on the part of the leaver, the interviewer can usefully be the leaver's immediate line manager. If the reverse is true it might be preferable to have some other manager or perhaps a skilled interviewer from the personnel or welfare departments.

But why bother to see someone who has given notice of leaving? Surely they have made their decision and it should be left to stand! On the contrary, although it may be a valued employee who is leaving, a considerable amount of useful information can be obtained and help given. Again, this will depend on the attitude of the leaver and the circumstances leading up to the termination. If the leaving is the end result of a series of abortive discipline interviews or of discharge, it would be asking for trouble to suggest an exit interview. However, if the notice to leave originated with the employee, there will almost certainly be value in discussing the position. Information may often emerge which may not otherwise have come to the surface.

I know of one manager who, when his secretary gave notice of leaving for what was obviously, even without probing, a considerable improvement in status, salary and responsibility, invited her out to lunch. It was described as a leaving lunch, but was originated with two other objectives in mind – to ensure that she really wanted to leave and that the new job was indeed all that it appeared to be, and to obtain some feedback about the company and/or relationships. After some initial hesitation on the part of the secretary, she told the manager some things about his behaviour which she had not previously had the courage to disclose. Fortunately they were not bad disclosures, but were sufficiently critical to make the secretary hesitate in telling the manager while she was still under the normal employment conditions.

This case reflects a relatively common state of affairs in which people who are leaving an employment are more likely to air their views than if they were continuing. The easing of constraints on them, real or imagined, encourages freer speech. Naturally this is good from the point of view of the employer who is seeking honest feedback, even though on occasions it can be embarrassing. Good management will not allow this opportunity of obtaining feedback, whatever the nature, to be neglected.

Objectives

The purpose of the exit interview might be to avoid the possibility of repetition of similar leavings in the future by determining the reasons, which may emerge as:

- comparison with other companies in terms of wages, conditions or progress

- a dearth of opportunities for highly qualified employees, perhaps because the company might be recruiting initially at too high a level
- organizational problems of which the company might not have been aware.

Consequently the specific objective of an exit interview is 'To determine the real reasons for the termination, with a view to rectifying any problems, organizational- or people-oriented, which might emerge'.

Pre-interview preparation

The interview arrangements are to a large extent in the hands of the employer's representative in terms of location and timing. This allows the interviewer time to prepare himself by

- finding out as much as possible about the work levels, progress, attitudes and behaviour of the interviewee
- determining whether there had been any previous moves to leave
- determining whether there had been any recent discipline or grievance action, and certainly
- confirming whether or not the company would want/be prepared to continue the employment if the notice were to be rescinded.

Otherwise, no special arrangements are necessary, the normal interview conditions prevailing.

Interview structure

The basic structure of the exit interview is very similar to that of the counselling interview in that the intention is to put the interviewee at ease and encourage him to talk openly about the reasons behind the decision to leave. It is possible that problems may emerge which, if solved, might result in a cancellation of the notice.

Consequently a substantial 'settling-down' process is essential, but not to the extent that the 'welcome' makes the interviewee feel ill at ease.

The next stage of the interview will be to allow the interviewer to express regret at the receipt of the notice and to state the purpose of the interview.

From this point the interviewer's role will change from leading the interview to allowing the interviewee to talk freely and openly about the reasons for leaving.

Once these reasons have emerged, the interviewee can be encouraged to express himself about the organization, the personalities and relationships in which he has been involved. It would be invidious to dig out 'dirt', but any relevant information which will improve the organization will be valuable.

When the information has been gathered, all that is left is for the interviewer to thank the individual for the information given and for his services during the employment.

Subsequent activity may be quite extensive, depending on the information extracted. It has to be assessed and analysed for value and veracity, and any action suggested from the comments made. Do not accept at face value everything which has been said; the views expressed must be examined and validated. Although on occasions such as this the leaver is more likely to speak out, unfortunately it may be done with malicious motives. When a series of exit interviews is conducted over a period, an image of the company and the treatment of its personnel is constructed which gives the opportunity for a valid assessment of problems.

Behaviours

Much of what has been said about interviewer's behaviours in counselling and appraisal will also relate to exit interviews. In general they will include:

- a lot of listening
- a lot of probing by way of open questions
- a lot of reflecting to encourage continued expression
- little personal talking except when essential
- little closed, leading or multiple questions
- little or no disagreeing (even with reasons), and certainly
- no interrupting or attacking, whatever the provocation.

If the objective of obtaining information which is helpful to the organization and its employees, present and future, is kept in the forefront of the interviewer's mind, the behaviours should come naturally, whatever the leaver might say.

This chapter has covered three types of interview over a progressive period of employment – the initial selection interview, the promotion interview and the exit interview. A common behaviour in all three is the use of probing questions to obtain information, usually of a deep level nature. Consequently the interviewer in all cases has to be listening for superficial answers which can be challenged. The different types of interviews provide a wealth of material from which their structure and behaviour can be planned.

Whatever the type, the interview must be conducted in the knowledge of the importance of the event to both the organization and the individuals. The interviewers must be highly skilled in both the technical and more subjective aspects of interviewing and comparing people objectively. A strong moral responsibility is placed on the interviewer who is usually in a very powerful decision-making position.

12 The appraisal interview

Many larger organizations have some form of annual appraisal of their employees. Some, like the Civil Service, include all employees; others include staff at a certain grade only; and there are numerous variations. The form of the appraisal varies in a similar way and range. At its most basic the boss has an annual 'chat' with each of the employees (or selected jobholders) in his responsibility level, with no formal note of the chat being produced and the resulting information decision being retained (or not) in the boss's head. Or a simple appraisal form outlining the individual's skill level and progress may be completed, but with no subsequent discussion; the management and/or personnel staff alone being aware of what is happening. The next stage on from this simple approach is one in which at one time I discovered I had been unwittingly involved – the completion of an annual report and appraisal form of a complex and comprehensive nature. However, not only the recorded information, but also the existence of the procedure is withheld from the person on whom the reports are being made. I am still intrigued by what might have been said about me at that time! At the other end of the spectrum in the more formal systems is, of course, the completion of a comprehensive appraisal form which is freely available to the person being reported upon.

From the basic approach, no discussion at all, the employee may be told what is contained in the report, sometimes with a variation that he is asked to comment on the assessment. It is more common that an opportunity is given to discuss fully the report with his boss, but on the strength of a description only, perhaps without full disclosure. The appraiser will inform the individual of the content of the report to the extent which is felt necessary or desirable, either from the point of view of the organization or the individual reporter. Ideally the report is made available in its entirety prior to an appraisal interview during which it will be discussed fully and openly. This would appear to be the only realistic method, but it does have some potential problems. One of these will be when the person reported upon is performing much less than satisfactorily and his receptivity to criticism is known to be at a low level.

The method currently in use by the Civil Service is a mixture of these approaches. There are two report forms – one which relates directly to performance during the reporting year against the objectives set at the end of the previous year is fully available to the person being reported upon. In addition to statements on the achievement of the objectives it includes sections on specific aspects and an overall assessment of performance. This open report form is given to the person being reported on who is asked to sign it as seen. The second form relates to promotability assessment with ratings on performance with that in mind. This form is not available to the person being reported on, although there is a right to be informed of the promotability assessment. Only the first report is discussed at the appraisal interview, although it is left to the discretion of the appraising officer to include verbal disclosure of the second form.

Annual pay increases are often included in the appraisal interview when discussing an individual's employment progression. In general this practice is not recommended because problems over pay can destroy any other good results achieved in the performance part of the interview. The same argument applies to discussion about promotion. I once interviewed a subordinate to whom I had given a very good performance report; discussion had gone well and many useful developments were agreed readily. But the positive nature of what had gone before was negated because I had to discuss the individual's promotion assessment which was, unfortunately, 'not recommended'. The interviewee did not and, even with extensive discussion, would not accept the validity of the recommendation and left the interview in a very sour state of mind, completely ignoring the very good performance rating. I have also experienced the reverse situation when I was on the receiving end of an appraisal.

AIMS AND OBJECTIVES

People at work need to know a number of essential (to them) items of information and opinion. Without this feedback an individual would be working in a vacuum at what may be an ineffective level or slowly regressing from an initial satisfactory level.

This need for feedback is based around the elements of security. If I am doing my job well and both I and my boss are aware of this (and I know that my boss is aware of it), I can feel reasonably secure in my job. To reach this stage I must be given the opportunity to achieve something and that achievement must be recognizable to others who will praise me. The achievements will bring me money, status, relationships, security etc. Many of these needs can be satisfied by self-assessment, but we also need the direct confirmation and support of others. To obtain this we must answer the following questions:

- What standards am I expected to attain in my job?
- Am I attaining those standards?
- What is the range of duties in my job?
- Am I performing at least satisfactorily in all aspects of this job?
- What personal attributes am I expected to demonstrate?
- Am I demonstrating them satisfactorily?
- Where do I go from here and how do I achieve this movement?

This is the minimum list of questions which should be addressed and answered during a job appraisal interview in which the aims are twofold:

- to establish the level of performance during the period under review and to seek ways of improvement
- to identify potential and means of development.

The more specific objectives for the interview can include:

- to agree with the interviewee the level of performance attained during the period under review
- to identify and discuss both strong and weak aspects of performance
- to agree methods of building on the strong and remedying the weak aspects
- to agree approaches and methods of training and development
- to agree job and personal performance objectives for the following review period.

The base of any appraisal interview should be the assessment of performance, judged by whatever means are felt to be appropriate, since the last review. This, however, does not mean that the appraisal interview is the only annual occasion on which the assessment is discussed with the worker. Rather it must be looked upon as the culmination of one part of a dialogue which should have been continuing throughout the review period. It is also the start of another part of this dialogue which will continue through the future period and will be concerned with the action necessary to fulfil the appraisal agreements.

It is easy to have these intentions, but in practice many events get in the way. Sometimes an appraiser will describe some poor quality which has come out of the blue as far as the interviewee is concerned, who may respond with: 'What are you talking about? You have never mentioned this before! Why didn't you say something at the time?'. The appraisal interview is not the occasion on which to drop thunderbolts on the interviewee, to castigate him about aspects which should have been brought out into the open at the time of the event. However, managers can always find excuses for not taking the relevant action at the appropriate time.

INTERVIEW STRUCTURE

As for most interviews, the basis of success in the appraisal interview is planning and preparation. The interviewer is in a strong position to prepare because he should have plenty of information on which to work.

Preparation

In order to make the interview as interactive as possible the interviewee must also have the opportunity to prepare. If the interview is arranged with at least a week's notice, this will give him time to consider

- what the interviewer is likely to say to him, and
- what he wants to say in relation to his performance, his training and development needs, and his ambitions for the future.

It is only fair to the interviewee to give him this time for preparation, rather than the only too common practice of the boss calling in the worker and saying 'By the way, I want to treat this chat now as your appraisal review. OK?' The worker *should* respond: 'Sorry boss, but this is an important event for me. I should like to have some time beforehand to think about it'. How often is this likely to happen with a boss who treats appraisal in this way? The approach tells us a lot about this boss-worker relationship!

The interviewee may be helped to prepare in a positive way by giving him a form which lists some useful topics for him to consider. These may include the following:

- In which events during the year was I pleased with my performance?
- Which events did not please me as far as my performance was concerned?

The interviewee can either bring the completed form with him to the interview or he can study it prior to the interview. Both these options would offer the opportunity of maximum preparation.

The interviewer will at the same time be doing his own

preparation. The following important items will be available to, or obtainable by the interviewer.

The job description. Although the boss will be aware of the job, he may find it useful to refer again to the job description to remind himself of its range etc. As time goes by additional items of work occur which without positive reference can be considered as integral parts of the job. Alternatively the interviewer may not be aware of all the complexities of the job and without this knowledge the interview can be difficult.

The objectives from the previous interview. During the previous year's appraisal interview, objectives for the ensuing year will have been set. The interviewer will need time prior to the interview to assess whether these objectives have been achieved. Of course, if a written report has been made, these aspects of performance will have been considered during its production. But the interviewer will still need to consider his attitude to these in order to express his views in the most appropriate way.

Action plan. In addition to the statement of objectives, a detailed action plan is often completed at the previous review. This plan will contain more specific and discrete aspects of action than those contained within the objectives. At this stage the interviewer can consider how far that plan has been completed and, if any items still remain, what further action might be necessary.

The report form. If the would-be appraiser has also completed the report form on the individual, he should know what has been included. However, some time may elapse between the completion of the report and the interview, so a study of what was written will help to refresh the appraiser's memory.

If the interviewer has not completed the report – it could be the boss's boss – he will certainly have to acquaint himself fully with its contents and question the person who completed the report about any points which are not completely clear and also about any aspects with which the interviewee is likely to take issue.

Whoever the interviewer, an important part of the preparation will be the decisions about which points must be raised and cleared, and how they will be approached and broached.

PHYSICAL ARRANGEMENTS

The physical arrangements for the interview will be similar to those for counselling and selection interviews. Privacy is obviously of prime importance and every effort should be made to ensure that the interview takes place in comfortable surroundings. Arrangements must be made to ensure that the interview is not interrupted either by physical presences or by telephone. In the former case, a simple notice fixed to the door of the interview room should suffice, and in most cases telephone calls can be intercepted – if not, the simple expedient of taking the receiver off its mount will remedy the situation.

Allow sufficient time to conduct the interview without pressure and to obtain as full a discussion on all aspects as is necessary. This is really saying that the interview should be as long as a piece of string! No interview as described can be conducted in less than half an hour, even where there is an excellent report on which the interview is based. In this instance, most of the interview will be concerned with future development and as this might be looking at a high level of achievement, the discussion may become complex. At the other end of the scale, no upper limit can be stated. I once shared an appraisal interview with an individual who was not at all happy with the performance review ratings given to him and far from happy with his promotion rating. This interview lasted 2½ hours at the end of which there was an adjournment for three days to allow the interviewee time to reconsider the situation and to make some developmental plans based on what had been discussed. The reconvened interview lasted a further hour – a total of more than 3½ hours.

Another, much shorter appraisal interview broke all the rules in the book. A member of my team had been pursuing a highly intensive training course programme away from our normal base. When he returned I was away running a course, so we saw each other only in passing. It was obvious that this situation would continue for a further two months, before the end of which an appraisal interview had to be performed. I had no concerns about the level of his appraisal – he was a highly skilled, very acceptable trainer, performing well above the norm for such training officers.

One Friday evening he called in the base office on his way home from a training event and as I happened to be there he offered me a lift home in his car since we lived reasonably close to each other. This seemed to be about the only opportunity which was going to present itself, so we agreed to hold the appraisal interview in his car as he drove me from the centre of London to the outskirts. Not the best of circumstances for an appraisal interview from any viewpoint, neither his nor mine, but in fact the only one possible.

I often wonder what would have happened if instead of the good report I had given him, there had been some bad news to impart. Presumably I would have had to walk from about half way!

STARTING THE INTERVIEW

Advice is often given to appraisers to set the interviewee at ease before settling down to the interview itself. As an interviewer I have encountered the greatest difficulty in finding anything which does not sound like a time waster, and as an interviewee I have become impatient when this technique has been practised on me. Many others with whom I have discussed this point agree that it is best to move into the interview immediately but smoothly.

Two items, however, which relate directly to the interview can be introduced as useful openers. The first, which is an information-giving behaviour by the interviewer, serves two purposes. A statement which describes the appraisal interview and what it is for, how the interviewer intends to conduct it and the desired active role of the interviewee ensures that the interviewee is fully aware of the implications of the event. But it also gives the interviewee a chance to settle down as he listens to the interviewer talking. But we don't want him to become too settled and let the interviewer do all the talking! So again we can start the interviewee talking by asking him what he hopes to achieve from the interview – information which can also be of use later, so it is far from wasteful talking.

PERFORMANCE REVIEW

At the performance review it would be simple for the interviewer to state how he views the performance of the individual. However, this may not be an appropriate approach, although at some stage the interviewer is going to have to state his case.

It may be preferable to ask the interviewee to describe how he sees his achievements and successes over the period, and also to comment on any events or processes where he was disappointed in his performance. From these two approaches an assessment of the achievement of the agreed objectives can be sought. During these comments by the interviewee, the interviewer must listen very carefully in order to react to any points or to make a mental note of those to which he may wish to return later.

This is one problem which may often arise in the interview. If some aspect is raised which is 'out of order' in the interview structure, should it be dealt with there and then or delayed until its 'correct' stage in the process? There is no golden rule about this. If it seems logical to deal with it immediately, do so, then return to the normal pattern. But if to do so would over-complicate the process, try to defer it to a later stage, acknowledging at the same time that the point has been noted. However, if this is the case, the interviewer *must* ensure that the item is considered before the end of the interview.

The novice interviewer may find it difficult to deal with

one or more out-of-course problems and then return to the process of the interview. The second approach may be more appropriate for the novice with the added reminder to return by making a specific note.

Usually during this stage of the interview the interviewee will make a realistic assessment of his achievements, in which case the interviewer will confirm this – normally a simple and pleasurable task. However, if the assessment is badly out of line from the correct position, the interviewer must be prepared to clarify this with the interviewee. It is important to try and avoid conflict between the appraiser and the interviewee. I do not say 'at all costs' as some advisers do, since the cause of potential conflict may be something which is incumbent on the appraiser to raise. In most cases conflict is produced not by *what* is said, rather *how* it is said and in this respect the interviewer should be completely in control.

The appraiser has to remember at all times that the appraisal is being made of the individual's performance and not of the individual as a person. Consequently reference should always be made to *what* the individual has done or said and the interviewer must be able to support these statements with factual evidence. This is particularly important in the next section of the interview.

ASPECTS OF PERFORMANCE

This is the part of the interview in which the interviewer and interviewee discuss, as necessary, specific items of the individual's performance. It is here that the dangers of over-personalization exist as mentioned above. Much will depend on what points are to be included in the review, but many problems may be avoided by concentrating on behaviour and actions rather than on personality interpretation.

For example, one aspect on which a report might have to be given could concern 'relations with colleagues'. This is a problem which will have to be raised at the interview. The first approach will be to encourage the individual to assess this aspect himself and in many cases an honest self-assessment will result. The problem can then be discussed and attempts made at agreeing solutions in a counselling approach. However, the interviewee may be unaware of or unwilling to face up to the fact that there is a problem. Whatever the case the situation must be discussed, and a tactful approach using the behavioural aspects is the one most likely to succeed. It would be most inappropriate to say 'You don't get on with people'. Responses to this may range from 'So what!', to 'I agree that I don't get on with you' or 'I don't agree with you'. The interviewer must try to avoid this sort of conflict and if there is an adverse reaction, should have actual cases to quote which will demonstrate the problem rather than have to state it brutally.

At one time I had a member of staff who had previously had reasonably good relationships with his colleagues, but these had started to deteriorate. He was unaware of any problem, but I had observed various incidents which demonstrated the superficial level of the problem. He played pool at lunchtime with his colleagues and he was quite a good player. However, whenever he lost, particularly to a less skilled player, he invariably left the room and went elsewhere for a period of time. On his leaving the comments emerged 'Oh, he's gone again. He must have lost.'. His reputation as a bad loser developed from this and the same attitude spilled over quickly into his work relationships. 'We had better not ask him to do this. He may not do it well at first, and then he's likely to give it up.'

The situation was deteriorating and I had to raise it with him at the appraisal interview which was then due. I asked him how he felt about his relationships. His response was that as far as he was concerned there was no problem. I then asked him whether he was aware of the references which were being made about him and why. He was completely unaware of them and was shocked by the revelation. He said that his actions were not at all as observed. When he wasn't playing (i.e. when he lost) he used the time in other ways until he could return to the table. We discussed how actions could be misinterpreted and their extension to the work area. He then said that he had noticed that he was being kept away from some aspects of work and could not understand why. Our discussion linked the minor effect of the pool room events with other aspects and he realized the implications. We then agreed on some activities which could help to remedy the situation – the first action, of course, was that he didn't walk out straight away if he lost!

FUTURE DEVELOPMENT

The historical part of the review has now been discussed and agreed and it is time to move on to the forthcoming year, in many ways the more important part of the interview. The following aspects will normally be included in this section.

Objectives. A plan for the year in as objective and quantitative terms as possible can now be agreed. The interviewee can be encouraged to say how he sees and wants his role to develop and the interviewer can supplement this with known future events which will have an impact on this role. As a result of this pooling of views, a realistic set of objectives can emerge.

Training. In order to achieve the agreed objectives the individual may need some remedial or developmental training. Consequently, part of the year's plan will include an agreed approach to learning/training.

Developmental needs. The planning process should not only be related to the needs of the organization; the development of the whole person should be considered. Therefore, any worthwhile plan will include agreed methods for assisting personal development. This might involve a career move during the year to widen the individual's work experience; a period of consolidation in the present job if this has recently been commenced; arrangements can be discussed for the pursuance of professional, technical or academic qualifications; or the engagement in additional, different work e.g. part-time projects.

Full discussion on these future events should take place, the interviewee contributing as much as possible to the finally agreed plan, rather than the appraiser.

TERMINATION

Once again the interviewer may find it difficult to finish the interview. This can be a real problem with people who are new to interviewing but this threefold approach may be found helpful.

1   The interviewer can summarize what has been discussed and agreed and either promise to produce an action note as a result of the interview or obtain the agreement of the individual for him to produce the note.
2   Ask the interviewee if there is anything he wants to ask or add to what has already been said.
3   Refer back to the start of the interview and the interviewee's objectives for the event. The interviewer then asks: 'Do you feel that the interview has succeeded in satisfying these objectives?' The answer to this question should be something like 'Completely'.

When these three items have been cleared, all that remains for the interviewer is to say 'Thank you and goodbye'. In practice the interviewer often starts to go over the ground once more, but if you are satisfied that you have obtained all the necessary information and that the interviewee is in the same position, close the interview in a positive manner.

SUBSEQUENT INTERVIEWS

It has been stated many times that realistic appraisal should be a continuing dialogue between the manager and the worker, over the period of the review, not just the annual review interview. However, there are many factors which prevent this ideal situation. A useful compromise can be a series of 'mini' appraisal interviews between the annual reviews. These could be held at three-monthly intervals to cover recent events. This would produce a system of an annual review followed by three mini-reviews, then the next annual review. This may not always be practical, but the minimum requirement should be one mini-review between annual reviews.

Mini-reviews are intended to be carried out at a much lower emotional level than the annual review, otherwise even a halfway review would not be feasible. There will not usually be a written assessment on which the appraiser would base the review. There should be, however, the action note which was produced at the end of the previous major review. This note is the logical starting point for the mini-review. Has all the planned action taken place? Which aspects have been completed and which ones remain for action? Why have the uncompleted items remained to this period of time? How can the remaining items be processed for completion?

One of the main advantages of the mini-review is that if action agreed previously is not taking place, even a six-month review will ensure that the failures are not left for as long as twelve months. The longer period could easily produce problems or exaggerate existing ones through non-execution. Once a mini-review system is established, it becomes much easier to plan and execute six-monthly reviews than for twelve months or longer. There will be some aims and objectives which will take longer than a three, six- or twelve-month period, but even these will benefit from a regular and fairly frequent review.

In addition to checking on the agreed action, the mini-review can also include a general review of performance over the period, particularly where improvement is sought. Without a documented report, the appraiser will have to reinforce any comments on performance with instances of behavioural evidence.

The third aspect of a mini-review will be concerned with the future progress before the next review, in terms of performance and individual development. It is a matter of choice whether a new action plan is agreed or any further items are added to the original plan; much will depend on the nature of the items.

DOCUMENTATION

Whether we are considering annual or mini appraisal reviews, it is essential in both cases that the interview details are recorded as soon as possible after the event so that any important agreements or decisions are not overlooked. A simple statement of subjects discussed, reactions and agreements reached is all that is necessary in addition to the summary nature of the specific action plan.

The action plan should preferably be short and simple, stating clearly the action agreed by both parties and the time period over which it should occur. The action must be completely clear and understood by both parties: the simplest method of ensuring this is for both the interviewer and the interviewee to read and sign the action plan to this effect. Both parties will then retain a copy as a reminder of the actions agreed.

BEHAVIOURS

A behaviour plan is essential for the appraisal review, perhaps more so than for many other types of interviews. It should include the following three decisions:

- to listen more than talk
- to seek the interviewee's view rather than impose one's own
- to encourage as much self-appraisal by the interviewee as possible.

Bearing these criteria in mind, the behaviour desired from the interviewee will be

- Giving views, feelings, opinions
- Testing understanding
- Proposing/Suggesting
- Supporting
- Disagreeing with reasons.

As suggested earlier, we will want the maximum amount of views and positive proposals to come from the interviewee. There will be occasions, however, when the interviewee will have to agree or accept the comments we make, but we should also welcome disagreement provided it is reasoned and rational.

In order to achieve this range of behaviour from the interviewee, the interviewer should exhibit the following behaviours:

- Giving information – limited and only as necessary
- Seeking views, feelings, opinions
- Testing understanding
- Seeking proposals, ideas, suggestions
- Building and supporting
- Suggesting rather than proposing, i.e. something like 'What do you think of the idea of taking over the whole of this area of work?' rather than 'You will do better to take over the whole area of work'
- Open
- Disagreeing – as little as possible but whenever necessary always with reason being stated

and as often as possible

- Summarizing.

Taking the message from the final comments, the appraisal interview is

- the culmination of a dialogue which has continued throughout the year
- not a singular, annual event
- an event which contains a review of the year's performance in both overall and specific aspects
- a discussion of objectives for the succeeding year

- a mutual discussion leading to agreement to action rather than an autocratic decision by the appraiser
- one in which the interviewee contributes more than the appraiser, and
- an effective and enjoyable experience even though it may not be all 'good' news.

13 The discipline interview

If we conducted a survey to determine which interview managers least enjoyed conducting, the answer would certainly be discipline or reprimand. Most people, even experienced managers, do not like reprimanding others and so have an antipathy to interviews of this nature. When they are undertaken, they are often conducted so ineffectively that the situation after is worse than before the event. Fashions in discipline change with leadership styles and other considerations and the manager of today must be fully aware of legislation applying to particular cases – and keep up with its ever changing demands. Some years ago the general flavour of management was highly autocratic and consequently the approach to discipline reflected this attitude. Discipline was synonymous with reprimand or discharge and employers could impose the latter in the knowledge that they had the absolute right to do so and that there was also someone else available to take over the work.

The phrase 'on the mat' had a real meaning in the days of extreme discipline. I can recall as a young man who had offended his management (by talking to a young lady employee during working hours) being taken to see the manager (first by my supervisor to the deputy manager then by the deputy manager to the manager). I was told to stand in front of the manager's desk on a small carpet or mat and after waiting at least three minutes while the manager kept on writing, I had to endure a five-minute tirade numerating my deficiencies and misdemeanours.

Naturally I was not asked for any comments which I might have to make in my defence, nor was I even asked for a guarantee that I would not wander again from the path of employee righteousness. I was simply told not to do so. I was then returned to the care of the deputy manager who repeated the reprimand, then to my supervisor who also repeated it, but in rather more earthy terms.

Did I ever repeat the 'misdemeanour'? Of course, but I made certain that I was not observed by any of the management! I did consider at the time that my treatment was harsher even than the Army from which I had recently emerged. At least when on a charge in the Army I was asked whether I had anything to say (even though any comments were obviously disregarded!).

With a change in general attitudes, aided perhaps by the onset of a period of low unemployment, a more benevolent managerial attitude began to emerge, had to emerge or was told to emerge. A discipline situation was seen to be an opportunity for rehabilitation and improvement of the offender rather than a reprimand alone which had doubtful improvement results. Of course, a reprimand if due has to be given, but a more caring approach is advocated. If this less one-sided and demanding attitude solved the immediate disciplinary situation and also gave the worker the opportunity and motivation (not through fear) to improve his performance, this was progress. The other benefit was that the employer could retain an employee who started to satisfy requirements rather than lose one who might be difficult to replace.

There is little doubt that this approach is generally more effective than the hard boot, although it is not a universally accepted method. It is perhaps with this more humane and successful attitude in mind that the administrators who foresaw a reduction in jobs and a consequent excess of labour looked to legislation. If the high unemployment rates of the bad years were to return, management might also revert to the less humane reprimand rather than rehabilitation. Consequently legislation was enacted which gave a measure of protection to workers who might err, principally by introducing a number of statutory steps to be followed before discharge from employment was allowed. Under the Employment Protection Act, a number of disciplinary interviews and warnings give workers time to improve before discharge is considered. Quite naturally there is also included in the legislation the right for an employer to discharge an employee immediately for certain infringements of the environmental rules, but the results of these infringements must be known beforehand to any employee.

This legislative protection does not govern the manner in which an individual conducts the discipline interview. Fortunately human relations in employment have progressed and employers now realize that the dictatorial attitude is more harmful to them than a more benevolent, regenerative approach. Consequently the latter occurs more frequently than the former.

COMMON FACTORS

There are different types of discipline interviews, depending on the stage the offender has reached in being a problem. However, some factors are common whatever the type of interview.

The interview should be conducted in private rather than demeaning the individual by 'telling him off' in public and preferably he must be aware beforehand of the nature of the interview. One can argue that this will give him time to think up excuses, but if the interviewer is absolutely sure of the facts these will carry no weight.

The interviewer has complete administrative control. He decides when and where the interview will take place, and to a large extent the atmosphere and the way in which it will be conducted. Consequently there should be full preparation and consideration of the approach, e.g. dictatorial, benevolent or rehabilitative.

PREPARATION

The principal element to be considered before the interview is the reason for the disciplinary action. This means that the interviewer must possess the full facts about the nature of the misdemeanour or, failing that, when it occurred, to what extent, who was involved, and so on. As far as possible these facts must be clear, absolutely conclusive and unarguable. If they are not, the interviewer has to decide whether he should in fact conduct an interview at all.

If the interview falls in the later stages of a disciplinary procedure, there must be no doubt at all about the evidence. If the facts are denied, the interviewer would be forced into a state of doubt.

If the interview is the first one with the individual, evidence may be less clear and the investigation may be more to determine blame or reasons. Such an interview would most likely go ahead even though doubts existed. The other type can only proceed if the evidence is conclusive: if it is not, and the interviewer 'knows' that the individual has done wrong, he may have to accept that disciplinary action cannot be taken at that stage.

In many cases the evidence for the misdemeanour or failing can be in irrefutable form and documented – or the lack of documentary evidence when something has not been done. Or the interviewer saw the event at first hand. Reported evidence is much more difficult, particularly when unsupported by others, and is therefore open to be refuted by the individual as victimization, error of interpretation or that it simply did not occur. Naturally the credibility of the reporter is relevant, but remember that internal credibility may not have the same weighting outside the organization or even inside other parts of it.

The golden rule, therefore is 'If in doubt, don't' even though you have a complete albeit subjective feeling about the case.

OBJECTIVES

The preparation period should also decide the manner in which the interview should be conducted. Two related factors will need to be considered:

- the stage of the disciplinary process
- the interview objectives

The objectives for the first interview or a singular event must be as follows:

1 To comment on the occurrence of the event
2 To determine why it occurred
3 To prevent a recurrence by that individual
4 To ensure development of the individual and therefore
5 To give the individual the opportunity to improve.

If the interviewer is not the first occasion of a problem with an individual, the objectives will be with a firmer intent:

1 To comment on the recurrence – words to the effect that 'You've done it again!'
2 To determine the reasons for the occurrence
3 To obtain agreement about future non-occurrence
4 To agree methods for preventing recurrence
5 To ensure that possible sanctions are understood
6 To give the opportunity to improve.

It may be that the individual has had more than one warning interview, but it is the policy of the organization to try everything possible to remedy a situation before taking the ultimate step of discharge. Consequently the objectives for a possibly penultimate interview would include:

1 To reprimand in no uncertain terms
2 To determine the reasons for the recurrence
3 To state final sanction action and ensure that the procedures are fully understood
4 To give the opportunity to improve.

METHODS AND STRUCTURES

The method of conducting the interview will naturally depend upon which stage of the discipline procedure has been reached, determined by the objectives set as described. In general terms the early interview, although still ensuring that a miscreant is aware that he has done wrong, has more the atmosphere of a counselling interview. As the procedure progresses, the interviews become more formal, although still helpful, until the penultimate stage when the reprimand must be the major item, linked with the warning. However, even in this latter case, there is still space for examining opportunities for improvements.

Let us look in a little detail at two discipline or potential discipline situations.

Correction

The first case is of a young office worker who has recently left school and this is his first job. He has been given a task to perform concerned with statistics which are important to the office. The construction of the statistics require continuous action during the period covered by the analyses. You are the manager and the reports have come through to you for signature and you see that they show results wildly different from the norm. From your certain knowledge you are aware that the statistics should have included particular items. Their omission causes serious errors in the analytical accuracy. The individual's line manager is absent owing to sickness so you have to take action to remedy the errors and you have decided to see the young man yourself.

Preparation. The principal activity prior to the interview must be to determine beyond any doubt what went wrong – this has been clearly identified; who was involved – the individual in question was the only one involved; and how the error occurred – your investigations have not given you any clear information.

In view of the circumstances of the individual's employment there is every indication that, although he caused the error, the real fault may not be completely his. Consequently the approach will initially be one of an investigatory nature, followed by a remedy if the fault was caused through lack of knowledge. However, you will also need to consider censure in case the reasons do not emerge as lack of knowledge, but rather of carelessness.

Other pre-interview considerations will be the usual ones of time allocation, privacy and the other physical requirements discussed previously.

Introduction. In view of the particular circumstances of the individual in this interaction, it may be necessary to have an extended introductory stage. Usually in discipline procedures both you and the interviewee will want to move quickly into the meat of the matter and generalizations will not only be superfluous but could raise the emotional level. However, in this case the individual is likely to be unsure, nervous, perhaps worried by having to meet his manager in a formal situation. Consequently, you may need an extended settling down period so that the interviewee is in the frame of mind to talk with some degree of confidence.

The obvious opener in this case would be to question the young person about his transition from school to work; the attendant problems; how he is seeing the job, and so on. If the questions, or at least the later ones, concentrate on the job and his reaction to it, there is the opportunity for a smooth lead-in to the next stage in which the problem is broached.

Information giving. This stage of the interview will have to be handled delicately, so that the interviewee does not immediately take offence as a result of an accusation or even an imagined one. Such an attitude would result in non-cooperation or, at worst, antagonism.

In this case it would be best to state simply the problem which has arisen and relate its incidence to the fact that this job was performed by the interviewee. Alternatively you could be more circumspect and approach the same point of questioning him about his knowledge of the work. Whatever you do it must be made clear at an early stage that

- the work he is doing is important which is why it is necessary for it to be accurate
- it is appreciated that he has been performing the work for only a short time and consequently nobody would expect him to know everything.

Investigatory. The statement of what has gone wrong will be followed quickly by a discussion aimed at clarifying the reasons for the error. Probably the most effective initial question will be of an open nature and could take the form of 'How do you think this error occurred?'. The response will depend on the knowledge of the interviewee. It may be that having the error pointed out will remind him of the action he should have taken. However, the more likely response will be one of ignorance of the event leading to the error.

In this case the interviewer must then move very firmly into the probing investigatory mode. Invite the individual to describe the path and process he followed in performing the task. At some stage, the interviewer, whose job at this stage is to clarify, probe and test understanding, would identify that part of the process which was being omitted or performed incorrectly. This identification would prompt further clarification that this was indeed the problem area and would allow the interviewee to complete the description of his process: more than one error might be occurring and the others may be missed if an incorrect assumption is made when the first error emerges.

Solutions. The natural progression from the question 'What is the problem?' and the response to it is 'What can we do about it? How can we remedy the situation?'

In many cases, certainly with experienced workers, the next step would be to seek ideas from the person involved as to how they would go about the revisionary process. This is based on the assumption that commitment would be greater if the solution orginated with the one who would have to implement it, particularly in cases of discipline. However, in this case it is most unlikely, because of the limited experience of the work, that the young person would come up with any realistic solutions. In spite of this it would still be useful to ask the question; a completely naive, unbiased mind might suggest something which would be overlooked by the more experienced.

When no ideas are forthcoming from the interviewee, the intervicwer must make proposals of his own for improvement, preferably in the form of suggesting rather than proposing. This gives the interviewee the chance to be involved even though the proposals are not his. The suggestion may not be for any form of training, but simply that more practice is necessary; or perhaps the task may be beyond the capabilities of the individual.

During the investigatory stages it may have been discovered that the omission occurred through carelessness or some other fault of execution rather than lack of skill. In such a case the solution will probably be a statement by the individual with a guarantee that there would be no repetition, whether this guarantee is sought by the interviewer or offered voluntarily.

Termination. Following on from this stage the interviewer should close with a summary of

• why the interview was necessary, and
• what action has been agreed.

You should include the first item of the summary because the later, longer part of the interview may have been developed into a counselling, advisory or development mode and it would be easy for the interviewee to forget the original reason for the event – an error. However, if the interview has progressed well, the interviewee will have learned something, will know what he has to do next, and will also know that he was to blame to some degree for an error or that an error initiated the event.

Discipline/correction

Where the circumstances differ from the case discussed the interview will take a rather different form although the structure is still basically the same:

- Preparation
- Introduction
- Information giving
- Information seeking and investigation
- Solution seeking
- Decision making
- Termination.

Let us take an example for this type of interview. The event concerns an experienced worker who has again done something for which he received an informal warning by his supervisor on the first occasion. In spite of its informality he was left in no doubt that it was a warning against repetition. The warning has apparently been ignored, the event repeated and the supervisor has passed the case to you for formal action.. The evidence of the occurrence is clear and you have confirmed this in your preparation.

The objectives for an interview of this nature are threefold:

1 To reprimand for the ignored warning
2 To discover any unknown factors
3 To take action to avoid repetition.

Although the evidence appears clear, this does not mean that the process of the interview will be straightforward. The alternatives can be presented in a flow chart form (see Figure 13.1).

Introduction. In this situation the interviewee is fully aware of why the interview is being held and its disciplinary implications. Therefore, it is most unlikely that a settling-in period will be necessary or desirable, both parties will be wanting to progress to the main part of the event. However, because of its nature, some interviewees may be in a high emotional state, probably evident from overt

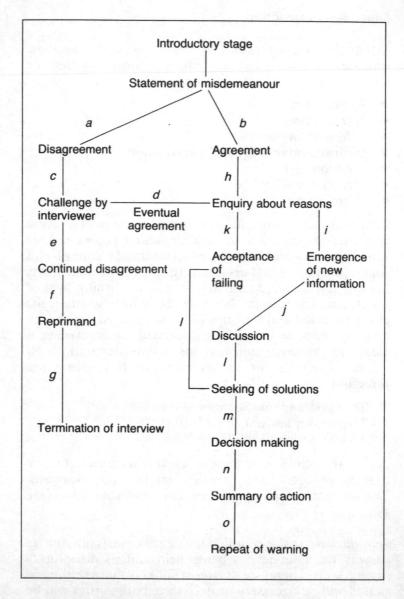

Figure 13.1   Progression of disciplinary interview

behaviour. The interviewer must be prepared for this, particularly if he knows the person well and can anticipate a particular behaviour pattern. If this is perceived to be the case there is little advantage in going ahead immediately with the interview. Not only because to continue would upset the interviewee even more, but little sense or openness would be achieved, agreements would not be so forthcoming and the interview might have little impact.

Therefore, if the signs suggest a delay of entry to the interview proper, the interviewer would be advised to acknowledge this and try to settle the interviewee into a less disturbed state. Once a reasonable level of stability is achieved by the interviewee, the interviewer can commence his predetermined plan of action. He must clarify at the outset the reason for the interview, i.e. the occurrence or in this case the recurrence of the misdemeanour following a previous warning, the seriousness of the recurrence and the implications of an interview of this nature.

The statement described must be comprehensive, but not long-winded, and the interviewee must be left in no doubt about your reaction to the recurrence.

Information seeking. There must then be no delay in moving the interview process over to the interviewee. This is done quite simply by posing the question 'What would you like to say about this situation?' or other words which are relevant to your style. It is at this stage that the alternative paths *a* or *b* in the flow-chart appear.

Although you are aware of the clear evidence, the interviewee may not realize this, or may feel that he can get away with it, or he may even deny it simply to be awkward. Whatever the motive, the interviewer must be in a position to deal with the denial. This refers back to the preparation in which the interviewer must ensure that he is aware of all the facts relevant to the event and is absolutely certain about what occurred. If there are doubts or uncertainties, it may be better that the interview does not take place. There is nothing worse in a disciplinary interview where the evidence is not available, than the individual denying the accusation and quoting his own 'clear' evidence that it is unjust.

But, as suggested, the event might be denied even where the evidence is absolute. The interviewer must have the courage of his evidence and reject the denial with firmness and conviction. The compelling statement will be a summary of the evidence which shows the truth of the interviewer's statement.

Even at this stage (*e* on the flow chart) the interviewee may still, illogically, deny the occurrence. He should have a chance to support his denial, but if the evidence is indeed clear, his statement should not have any credence.

The interviewer must not enter into an argument with the interviewee over this denial. If he knows his case is correct, the interviewee must be told clearly and unemotionally that this is so and the denial cannot be accepted. The interviewee (path *f*) may want to continue the disagreement, in which case the interviewer must state the reprimand and warning against further recurrences and then terminate the interview. Obviously, this is unsatisfactory, but where the evidence is indisputable, the interviewee has been given the right to speak and to realize that denial is not supportable, there is no other realistic course of action.

In most cases, however, the individual will either agree straight away with the statement or, having seen that the evidence is against him, will ultimately agree.

The abnormal flow path *a, c, d* will now join the more normal progression in which the interviewee, having heard the stated reason for the interview, agrees and responds realistically to the invitation to speak.

The interviewee has two options open at this stage. He can either accept the situation and plead no mitigating circumstances, or he can give some information on a related incident about which the interviewer knew nothing. If the discipline was for lateness there may have been some unforeseen problem over car-sharing, or an accident which delayed the traffic longer than one would reasonably expect, and so on. I once had to interview a young lady on a subject which was not related to discipline. She was very late and I was on the point of writing off the interview, particularly as I knew she had a bad record for attendance. But she eventually arrived and took the wind out of my sails by recounting a traumatic experience. She had set out in ample time to arrive at the appointed hour and was waiting at the bus stop. As the bus drew up, right in front of her someone threw themselves under the bus. She was so shaken by this incident that she had to be taken to hospital and consequently was late. We can never be 100 per cent certain we are in possession of all the facts.

Solution seeking. Whether or not additional information has emerged, the next stage of the interview is to prevent a recurrence of the problem. If there was to be a further recurrence the disciplinary situation would obviously be exacerbated.

It may be that a solution was agreed at a previous interview, but the individual for whatever reason did not comply. The solution should be confirmed and the individual firmly committed to following it, or, if necessary, a new solution sought.

New information may necessitate the production of a new solution or a modification of the original one. Whatever the case, the onus must be on the individual to suggest a solution to which he will be committed. Only as a last resort should the interviewer impose the solution, at least seeking a response to a suggestion before taking this action.

Agreement must then be reached on the solution, to which must be added a warning about failure to observe, the possible penalties and time limits involved.

Termination. At this stage there should be no doubt that the interview has been of a disciplinary nature. This will be confirmed with a summary of the reasons why it had to be held, the action agreed in the counselling stages and finally a reiteration of the time limit for improvement which must be included in any action plan. After all, if earlier interviews were indeed to prevent recurrence, this one is very firmly for the same reason, or the interviewee will have to pay the ultimate price.

AFTER THE INTERVIEW

Legislation requires written records to be maintained of disciplinary interviews and at certain stages of the procedure the interviewee must be given a copy of these records. But commonsense and good management dictates that this action should be taken without any enforcement regulations. Memories are short or selective, and if a matter is raised some time later, there may be a difference of opinion. A written record solves this problem. If action is agreed, both the interviewer and the interviewee should have a copy – in later stages this is mandatory – so that there is no possibility of confusion as to what has to be done, by whom and by when. Where the problem results in discharge, which may produce an industrial tribunal hearing, written records are essential.

The minimum record must include

- Date of interview
- Names of interviewer and interviewee
- Reason for interview
- Agreed action by both parties
- Details of the consequences of non-improvement within the agreed time.

The later, more formal interviews require that copies of the record are signed by the interviewee as evidence of having seen and agreed its contents.

Other entries can include the principal items discussed before agreement was reached and comments, necessarily subjective, about the interviewee's attitude and reaction to the interview.

Where the action plan has a time-limit involved, the procedure should be reviewed during its course. This interview may be either a further disciplinary measure if the necessary progress has not been made or a confirmatory one with a counselling element if all has gone well. It is as essential to hold an interview to confirm progress as it is to continue discipline.

Review should not be delayed until the end, particularly if the probation period is a long one. Informal reviews are useful and at least one formal review is necessary to ensure that all attempts at improvement are being made, an assessment of what has been achieved and a general assessment of progress made so that the person knows exactly where they stand. It is unfair on the other person to let him fall unchecked and then to use this as a weapon at the next stage interview.

All these activities suggest that the interviewer is not playing the role of disciplinarian alone. Most people with problems require counselling and advising and react well to it, rather than being ruled with a rod of iron. But the person in charge must also impose sanctions and discipline if the helping, caring approach is ignored or rejected.

14 The grievance interview

Grievance interviews often have the same effect on managers as discipline interviews. Not because they are similar, in fact they are almost poles apart, but because they are regarded as difficult events, which can produce conflict between the interviewer and interviewee.

The obvious difference between the discipline and grievance interview is that the former is manager-initiated whereas the latter is almost always interviewee-initiated. Perhaps in this respect the grievance interview is more allied to the counselling interview than any other.

The principal similarity between the discipline and grievance interview is that they both involve emotional, perhaps over-emotional, reactions to the detriment of objectivity and good management. Consequently the counselling element in the grievance interview has similarities with counselling, discipline and appraisal interviews.

Usually the individual knocks on the boss's door and asks to be seen because he has a complaint. The manager must be prepared

- to invite the person in straight away
- to insist on a delay in holding the interview
- to refuse to accept the request.

Let us take the latter option first. It would be most unwise for any manager to refuse to listen to an employee's grievance. In fact, by law, there must be a mechanism for grievance procedure. Usually the grievance will be taken to the person's next line manager. However, this step can be omitted if the grievance relates to the immediate manager or if the person with the grievance specifically rejects this option. The grievance procedure of an organization gives employees the right to take grievances to the highest level in that organization.

The basic principle of dealing with grievances, as far as the management is concerned, is that they should be as immediate as possible and at the lowest relevant level. Experience has shown that the higher an unresolved grievance is taken, the more intransigent becomes the person with the grievance and the more difficult it is to be solved. In the line process the problem often lies with the manager in that line.

OBJECTIVES

The objectives for a grievance interview are relatively simple and straightforward:

1 To listen to and understand the nature of the grievance
2 To take action to resolve the grievance
3 To ensure that the circumstances producing the grievance cannot be repeated
4 To assist the person with a grievance to follow any other procedures necessary.

The person to whom the problem is taken must be able to treat grievances sympathetically and with an open mind because of the possibility that they are part of the problem.

STRUCTURE

Preparation. Other than knowledge of how to conduct an interview of this nature, there is little the interviewer can do to prepare himself for the event. Whatever his mental state preceding the interview, his attitude must be one of positive reaction and acceptance of his role in the event.

This will depend on whether there is an immediate or delayed acceptance of the request for an interview.

Where the manager agrees to see the person straight away, his commitment to the interview must be total and whatever task was being performed should be put to one side. The only preparation is the decision to react positively to whatever may emerge.

However, at the time the interview is requested, it may not be possible to accept immediately, in which case an appointment must be made with the shortest possible delay. A delay will usually only exacerbate the problem for the person with the grievance because the 'hurt' will fester, so postponement must be the last resort. But it can sometimes help the interviewer, particularly if he has a good internal grapevine, or an assistant who can tactfully identify the problem during the delay. At least if the nature of the problem is known, the interviewer is not at a complete disadvantage when the interview starts.

Of course, where the interview has to be delayed, there is nothing to stop the interviewer from asking the reason for the request. A common response may be: 'I'd rather wait until we meet before I say anything!'. Interviewer beware – the problem is usually very serious when this sort of answer is given.

Introductory. This is not the occasion to indulge in social chitchat and the person with the grievance is unlikely to want or even allow it. His only interest is the grievance. Consequently the introductory stage is also the start of the *investigatory* stage. The interviewer's opening remarks, once the person is seated will be the risky, but essential, invitation 'Right Fred/Nellie, tell me what the problem is'.

In most cases this invitation will open the flood gates and the problem will come pouring out. The role of the interviewer at this stage is to listen intently and sift out the obvious facts from emotions clouding the issue. The longer the person talks, the more likely will be a reduction in the emotional temperature as the grievance comes 'off his chest'. It may be helpful to encourage this process with questions and reflections even when the issue is clear.

Once the initial complaint is unloaded and the interviewee is in a more settled state of mind, the real probing questions can be posed with a reasonable chance of being answered objectively. This can continue until the interviewer is content that all the relevant information has emerged and/or the interviewee has composed himself.

Resolution. At this stage the interview can evolve into a discussion between the interviewer and interviewee, rather than a monologue by the person with the grievance. The aim will be to resolve the problem, or at least identify possible actions or solutions. This book has previously stressed that the solutions should be sought from and posed by the interviewee rather than the interviewer. However, in this type of interview that approach may not be relevant, particularly where the problem may be caused by the interviewer.

There will be instances when a resolution will not be necessary. As in counselling situations, sometimes the problem is resolved simply by the person expressing his views, and he may be quite satisfied to let the matter drop or realize that there was no real grievance. On the other hand there may have to be a further reference up through the grievance procedure. A written statement of the grievance should then be sent to the next relevant line manager.

Conclusion. Again the most effective conclusion is for the interviewer to summarize the agreed action. But although the interviewer is usually pleased that the event is over he must not forget to thank the interviewee for bringing the grievance to his attention. This expression must be sincere. If the grievance had not been exposed, the manager would have been unaware of the problem, perhaps one of his own making.

There is no doubt that discipline and grievance interviews are not the interviewer's favourite events, but they are unavoidable. The pain on both sides can be considerably reduced by an efficient and humane approach: efficient in that the interviewer is able to control the structure of the interview in such a way that both parties have the opportunity to put their case; humane in that the interviewer recognizes the rights of the other person and behaves accordingly.

This philosophy should be common to all interviews and adherence to the most efficient, effective and humane methods will go a long way to making them enjoyable and productive events for both interviewer and interviewee.

Recommended reading

Anstey, E., *An Introduction to Selection Interviewing*, HMSO, 1977.

Argyle, M., *Social Interaction*, Methuen, 1969.

Argyle, M., *The Psychology of Interpersonal Behaviour*, Penguin, 1972.

Berne, E., *What do you say after you've said Hello?* Corgi, 1975.

Berne, E., *Games People Play*, Penguin, 1980.

Buzan, T., *Use your Head*, BBC Publications, 1982.

Dewey, D.M., and McDonnell, P., How to be Interviewed, BIM, 1980.

Fletcher, C., *Facing the Interview*, Unwin Paperbacks, 1981.

Fletcher, J., *The Interview At Work*, Duckworth, 1973.

Fraser, J.M., *Employment Interviewing*, MacDonald & Evans, 1966.

French, D., and Seaward, H., *Dictionary of Management*, Gower, 1983.

Goodworth, C.T., *Effective Interviewing for Employment Selection*, Business Books, 1983.

Gough, J.S., *Interviewing in 26 Steps*, BACIE, 1981.

Harris, T.A., *I'm OK You're OK*, Pan, 1973.

Higham, M., *Coping With Interviews*, New Opportunity Press.

Honey, P., *Face to Face*, 2nd edn, Gower, 1988.

Honey, P., *Solving People Problems*, McGraw-Hill, 1980.

Honey, P., and Mumford, A., *Manual of Learning Styles*, Honey, 1982.

James and Longeward, D., *Born to Win*, Addison-Wesley, 1971.

Kolb, D.A., and Fry, R., 'Towards an Applied Theory of Experiential Learning', in Cooper, C.L. (ed.) *Theories of Group Processes*.

Kolb, D.A., Rubin, I.M., and McIntyre, J.M., *Organisational Psychology: An Experiential Approach*, Prentice-Hall, 1974.

MacKay, I., *A Guide to Asking Questions*, BACIE, 1983.

MacKay, I., *A Guide to Listening*, BACIE, 1985.

Philp, T., *Making Performance Appraisal Work*, McGraw-Hill, 1983.

Plumbley, P.R., *Recruitment and Selection*, IPM, 1974.

Rackham, N., Honey, P. et al., *Developing Interactive Skills*, Wellens, 1971.

Rackham, N., and Morgan, T., *Behaviour Analysis in Training*. McGraw-Hill, 1977.

Rae, W.L., *The Skills of Training*, Gower, 1983.

Rae, W.L., *The Skills of Human Relations Training*, Gower, 1985.

Randell, G., Packard, P., and Slater, J., *Staff Appraisal*, IPM, 1984.

Rodger, A., *The Seven Point Plan*, NIIP, 1971.

Shouksmith, G., *Assessment through Interviewing*, Pergamon Press, 1968.

Stewart, V. and A., *Practical Performance Appraisal*, Gower, 1977.

Stewart, V. and A., *Managing the Manager's Growth*, Gower, 1978.

Whitaker, P., *Selection Interviewing*, The Industrial Society, 1973.

Index

closed 25, 26
Kipling's honest men 32
leading 30
multiple 27
multiple choice 29
non-question 30
open 31
testing understanding 33
what, where, who, when, why
    and how 32
Questioning
    purpose 24
    techniques 24

Recording of practice
    interviews
    audio 119
    video 119
Reflecting behaviour 36
Reprimand interviews 186
Role playing 117

Seating 13
    positions 13
Seeking information 108, 109
Selection interviews 156
    behaviour planning 161
    discussion level 162
    introduction 156
    job analysis 151
    job information 158
    job specification 150
    post-interview 160
    planning 156
    structure 156
    termination 159
    winding-up 159

Selective listening 53
Seven-Point Plan 121, 152
Seven Stage planning model 96
    aims 100, 102
    behaviours
        interviewee 106
        interviewer 106
    issue review 97
    Key Success Factors 103
    methods of achieving success
        105
    review
        self-questioning 110
Special abilities 124, 154
Special aptitudes 124, 154
State of body 52
State of mind 52
Structure 20
Suggesting behaviour 42, 109
Summarizing behaviour 39, 109,
    110
Supporting behaviour
    42, 108, 109, 110
Task analysis 151
Telephone interruptions 12
Termination 159
Testing understanding 33
Training interviews 114

Value judgements 70
Verbal signals 60
Video programmes
    interactive 115
Viewpoints 18, 65

Winding-up interviews 159
Work attainments 153